WAR AND REFLECTION

THE NAVY AIR CORPS: 1944 - 1946

REFLECTION ON WAR FIFTY YEARS LATER

Walter W. Benjamin

RED OAK PRESS
White Bear Lake, Minnesota

**War and reflection -- The Navy Corps 1944-1946
Reflection on War Fifty Years Later**

Copyright   1996 by Walter W. Benjamin

All rights reserved. No Part of this book may be used or reproduced in any manner whatsoever without written permission except brief quotations in critical articles or reviews.
For information address Stan Hill, President, Red Oak Press, P.O. Box 10614, White Bear Lake, Minnesota 55110-0614.

Printed in United States of America
99 98 97 96   10 9 8 7 6 5 4 3 2 1

Cover Design and Art: Mary Coughlin and Steve Harmon
Editor: Douglas C. Benson
Copy Editor: Doris H. Hill
Printer: Bethany Fellowship
Photo: Back Cover: Linda J. Mc Nary
Library of Congress Catalog Card Number 96-70760

**Benjamin, Walter W. 1926
    War and Reflection**

   Includes bibliography, index and table of contents.

1. Autobiography   2. Philosophy
3. Ethics   4. World War II
5. History

ISBN 0-9640439-1-2

These reflections are dedicated specifically to those citizen soldiers of Pipestone, Minnesota, and more generally, all of those from "Our Towns" across the American heartland who fought for freedom in the Second World War and subsequent wars as well as those presently at the battlements guarding freedom across our world.

"The mystic chords of memory, stretching from every battlefield and patriot grave to every living heart and hearthstone all over this broad land, will yet swell the chorus of the Union when again touched, as surely as they will be by the better angels of our nature." *--Abraham Lincoln, First Inaugural Address*

"Civil courage . . . can only grow out of the free responsibility of free men." *--Dietrich Bonhoeffer, 1942*

"It is well that war is so terrible--we would grow too fond of it." *-- Attributed to Robert E. Lee*

Table of Contents

War and Reflection

Preface 7
Introduction 11
1. Leaving My Cocoon: Stepping Into Manhood 17
2. The Great Disappointment 22
3. Boot Camp: A Demanding Discipline 25
4. Radio and Radar Readiness 43
5. From Shotguns to Machine Guns 51
6. Preparing For Combat 57
7. Military Melancholy 65
8. Radioman To Rails 71
9. Airman To Academia 83

II WAR AND REFLECTION: A HALF CENTURY LATER 87

Introduction 89
10. 1960s Vignettes of Campus Culture: I 95
11. 1960s Vignettes of Campus Culture: II 113
12. Is the Warrior a Barbarian? 129
13. The Enduring Allure of War 135
14. Love: War's Ally and Foe 141
15. The Military as Family 147
16. The Warrior and the Pacifist 155
17. The Case for Universal Military Service 163
18. Do Intellectuals Have Blood On Their Hands? ... 178
19. Hiroshima, Truman, and Revisionist History 191
20. Sociobiology: Is Violence Sown in Our Genes? ... 203
21. The Churches' Failure of Moral Guidance During Desert Storm 213
Conclusion 223
Bibliography 230
Index 236

Acknowledgements

I would like to extend my appreciation to my editor, Doug Benson; my compositor, Erin Dwyer; my copy editor, Doris Hill; my graphic arts consultant, Mary Coughlin; my artist, Steve Harmon; and my secretary, Pat Burt. All of these dedicated people have contributed their expertise to make *War and Reflection* a quality book.

I am especially indebted to my publisher, Stan Hill, President of Red Oak Press for his yeoman service and attention to detail in this book. I am grateful for both his friendship and his knowledge of the publishing business that he has freely extended to me.

Walter W. Benjamin

Preface

For the majority of the men of my generation, the Second World War was the defining event in the shaping of their personal identity. From 1941 through 1945, approximately 20 million citizens served America in places both familiar and strange. Whether these warriors volunteered or were drafted, the call to arms and the struggle to destroy tyranny tore them abruptly from their families, spouses, and children. For those just out of high school, such as myself, military service was a memorable rite of passage. It expanded and deepened the interval between adolescence and adulthood. It broke open the cultural cocoons in which those from the insular "Our Towns" across the heartland had slumbered. While the great drought of the 1930s drove tens of thousands of Oakies from our southern plains into California, the wartime 1940s set in motion a massive physical and cultural dislocation of millions across America and the world. The United States was changed forever.

Like other teenagers, I entered the Navy Air Corps as a boy and emerged a man. I did not see combat, yet was tested in ways that I would not have been tested had I remained a civilian. I gained ground on myself. I broke the restricting bonds of an authoritarian father and gloried in the liberty of being out from under his paternal hand. But, while I enjoyed the new freedom that the Navy Air Corps provided, I also came to realize that my family's discipline was rooted firmly in its love. My moral code--carefully crafted by parents, village elders, church, and school--was put to the test. I had to defend and practice the principles I had been taught.

The cultural and moral options available to me in the dozens of Vanity Fairs that I traversed challenged my values. I confronted choices unavailable to those who lived in communities whose distance from the fray left custom unchanged and unchallenged. But besides temptation, testing, enticement and a world of strange-sounding names and places, the military provided maturation, friendship, and leadership. I have never considered, therefore, that my military sojourn between high school and college represented "lost years." Rather, it was the threshold to a more sober, prudential, and productive life in college, graduate school, and beyond.

The stream of reflections that follows flows from three sources:

1) Long and serious study; as a history major in college and graduate school, I took courses on the twentieth century and World War II, and subsequently I have continued to read deeply and have published in that field.

2) Experiences--the German word is *Geschichte* rather than *History*--that were existential, traumatic and deeply individual.

3) Wartime correspondence; my Mother kept a treasure trove of almost 250 letters that I wrote while I served in the Navy Air Corps. Each letter had been neatly scissored open, read, passed along to other members of the tribe of Benjamin, returned, and finally tucked away carefully and lovingly in a box, in chronological order. In addition to the letters themselves, my Mother saved items I had enclosed with them: photos of our crew and plane, diagrams of radios and radar, jokes, and cartoons. Also saved were the programs from every divine service I

attended, either on or off base, and the Navy menus for special occasions. I enclosed these with my letters to assure my family that, although I was far away, I was attentive to the needs of both my body and soul.

Fortunately for posterity, long-distance telephone calls were expensive, difficult, and therefore rare during the war years. I wrote about two or three letters a week to my parents, my two brothers and sisters, aunts and uncles. When we needed instant communication for either good or bad news, we used Western Union telegrams. I sent five of them during my two years of service.

At home, after Sunday dinners my parents required my brother, Roger, and two sisters, Martha and Mary, to write to Bob and me before reading the Sunday funnies. Unfortunately, few of the letters I received from them or from my parents survived. Like many young people, even those living in wartime, I then lacked a sense of history, family connectedness, and the importance of preserving the thoughts in those letters for the generations to come.

Written on Naval Air Corps stationery, my communiques are short, 350-500 word, one-page epistles. They detail the days' events, struggles, successes, friends, aircraft and liberty. I often ask for news about Pipestone, the family, and my high school friends in the service. Invariably upbeat, they always end with "Your son, Neb," a nickname from childhood years. After 50 years the pages are brown around the edges and many are worm-eaten. But the letters' condition is not what is important, any more than the misspellings and grammatical errors I scattered through them like a child sprinkling cinnamon on hot buttered toast. What is important is that they represent what a legion of lads of my generation experienced.

A word about rhetoric. My writing is not presently "politically correct"--I use traditional pronouns for Homo Sapiens and the Deity. I believe the penchant for gender-neutrality makes a fetish of linguistic faddishness. Like past classical authors of the magnificent English literature tradition, when I use the term "man" or "men," I am, of course, inclusive and mean generic humanity and all humankind.

It will be clear to the reader after a few pages that I have great admiration for the warrior. These reflections, therefore, are dedicated to those who served their country in my generation, as well as those presently at the battlements guarding freedom across our world.

Introduction

By the time I entered our nation's military service, the Second World War had been raging for five years. It began when Hitler's Panzers smashed into Poland on September 1, 1939. Even before that momentous event, however, there was a long series of events during the 1930s that foreshadowed the second international conflagration of the century. With growing impunity and arrogance, Hitler took Germany out of the League of Nations, pinched off the Saar, and occupied Austria, the Sudetenland, and finally the rest of Czechoslovakia. He protested he needed *lebensraum*, enough space to accommodate all Germans in neighboring states. The Spanish Civil War, from 1936-39, served as a testing ground for the military technology Germany and Italy would use against the USSR. Redivivus, too, was Mussolini's fantasy of the rebirth of the Roman Empire. Photos of his brutal attack on Ethiopia, a country barely out of the Stone Age, showed planes strafing natives whose only available response was to throw spears. Hemingway wrote movingly in *A Farewell to Arms*, of his experience as an ambulance driver on the Italian front during World War I. Nonetheless, his message of cynicism and the nihilism of human existence had not served to rally the democracies to strengthen their battlements.

In the Orient, Japan, like Germany, was seizing more space, calling its conquests "The Greater Asian Co-Prosperity Sphere." Japan had invaded Korea, long the doormat and stepping stone between China, Japan, and Russia, and had taken over Mongolia and the eastern seaboard cities of China. Japanese bombs had killed sailors on the U.S. gunboat, *Paney*, on patrol in the Yangtze River. A mild protest was our only response. Although the rays of the Japanese imperial sun turned south and burned with ever increasing intensity, we continued to sell her mountains of scrap iron. Later, Americans would see that scrap in Japanese battleships, tanks, torpedoes, bombs, and shells.

With the clarity that comes with hindsight, by 1939 it was easy to see that we had long been on the slippery slope toward war. Anyone even faintly acquainted with human nature and the predatory character of ethnic and tribal collectives could see that Homo Sapiens was hardly the angelic and altruistic creature that 19th century social thinkers had thought him to be. Later, history would commend Franklin D. Roosevelt for his political sagacity in detouring around the pacifists, isolationists, and "America Firsters." But at the start of World War II the "doves" were legion and included the national hero turned appeaser, Charles Lindbergh, and countless mothers who cried, "We did not raise our sons to be killers." Millions thought we could simply pull the drapes across the Atlantic and the Pacific and hunker down and tend our North American homestead.

Roosevelt knew Hitler to be a crazed Aryan monster whose Fascist stompings were laying waste the long-husbanded and carefully tended garden of Western culture. Hitler's submarine packs roamed the Atlantic, intent on strangling the United Kingdom, the sole remaining obstacle to the triumph of the Third Reich. Roosevelt also knew that simply averting our eyes or dropping to our knees would be disastrous, and so he skillfully set out to change the opinion of the isolationist heartland. His statecraft finally convinced us to see that when a barbarian is destroying a neighbor's plantation, it is one's duty to lend a hand. In 1940, with the foundations of Western Civilization in jeopardy, against stubborn congressional opposition and a vociferous pacifism, FDR provided Lend-Lease for England and gave her 100 old destroyers.

World War II was an unnecessary war. The supreme irony is that pacifism helped create that war, and its conclusion was brought about by the most destructive weapon in history--the atomic bomb--produced from the research of a pacifist, Albert Einstein.

Two very different visions of war and peace have coexisted in the Western world for at least two centuries. One vision sees peace as being accomplished and maintained through disarmament and the compromise of international differences. This position, which has long been held by much of the Western intelligentsia and is symbolized by Neville Chamberlain, says, "Speak softly and carry a very small military stick." Long-forgotten international conferences based on this view, held at Geneva, Locarno, and Lausanne during the 1920s, generated pious agreements and the illusory hope that peace is preserved by high-sounding words and impressive signatures on parchment.

The opposite vision sees peace as being primarily a result of successfully deterring war. The Romans recognized that "no peace keeps itself." John Jay wrote in *The Federalist*, "Nations will make war whenever they have a prospect of getting anything by it." The first vision dominated our statecraft between the two world wars. The result? The U.S. became one of the most completely disarmed great nations in history. The total number of American military personnel on active duty fell below a quarter of a million in the early 1930s--and kept falling. The army's budget was sliced in half in 1934 to help finance New Deal social programs. The American army was smaller than the armies of 15 other nations, including Greece and Portugal. Some American troops still trained with wooden guns and mock-ups of tanks and cannon as late as 1941.

If pacifism prevented war, there would never have been a Pearl Harbor.

We should never forget how close the Western democracies came to being defeated--or what a horror it would have been for the entire world if they had lost. We should never forget the policies and illusions that brought the Western nations to the brink of catastrophe. Those illusions, which today are often mixed with a barely concealed hostility to Western civilization, have spawned an extensive coterie of revisionist historians. This new breed tends not only to overlook the historic achievement that saved our civilization, but is intent on denigrating the West in general and excoriating the United States in particular. Symbolic of this mind-set have been the annual pilgrimages to Hiroshima and Nagasaki to denounce the dropping of the atomic bomb.

The fiftieth anniversary of the end of World War II has come and gone, but we should never forget that the reason this war became necessary was that democratic nations left themselves dangerously vulnerable. The cost of such vulnerability is, of course, even greater in a nuclear age.

From 1941-1945 millions of youngsters, I among them, were subjected to a regimen of external discipline that in time became internalized. Decades after the war, many servicemen still wore their boots, jackets, and fatigues, not only because of their quality, but because they had become a talisman attesting to a unique and communal experience.

During World War II millions of servicemen were spread across America and the world. We encountered new ways, new food, new friends, new customs, and new mores. In the Navy I learned to distinguish between a dozen different dialects of the English language--seven from the Atlantic seaboard alone. I made friends from every corner of the United States. After the war many of us sought jobs in places we had visited while we were in the service.

The G.I. Bill, moreover, was the best anti-poverty measure our nation has ever devised. Legions of ex-servicemen who had neither considered nor had the means of going to college, had the opportunity to be the first in their families to achieve a bachelor's degree. It was a break-out experience for many who otherwise had little opportunity but to take up their father's lunch pail and trudge off to the mill or the mine. Moreover, veterans forever changed the collegiate atmosphere. Their discipline, maturity, and seriousness curtailed, at least temporarily, the superficialities of freshman hazing and the *Animal House* antics of fraternities.

Speaking personally, psychic maturation was the most beneficial consequence of my having been in the military. Fortunately, a "just war," (Justem bellum) provided me with a time to tread water between an excessively long adolescence and the demands of college. I graduated from high school at the age of 17 and was unprepared to undertake the rigors of collegiate life. A classic late bloomer, I needed more time to separate both physically and psychically from my Father and decide upon a career.

My Navy experience came at exactly the right time. The military provided me with opportunities and responsibilities that civilian life could not match. Had I experienced combat, the major share of the responsibility for our Privateer's radio and radar operation would have fallen on my shoulders. The protection of our vulnerable rear was also my obligation. With the onset of peace and at the age of 19, as a Navy policeman, I was responsible for the processing and discipline of hundreds of military personnel on transcontinental trains.

The military assumes the maturity of its members and grants them serious responsibilities earlier than does the civilian sector.

"The Marines are looking for a *few good men*" is more than just a recruiting slogan.

One

Leaving My Cocoon: Stepping Into Manhood

During my high school years I followed the war's military and naval campaigns with adolescent intensity. I had turned from cops- and-robbers and cowboys-and-Indians to imagining those Aryans and yellow men who would soon be my adversaries. As a boy I was overwhelmed with untested illusions of omnipotence and dream-fantasies. For psychological balance, warriors, even warriors-to-be, must portray their enemy either as super-human or sub-human. This defense mechanism excuses one from violating the commandment, "Thou shalt not kill," because one is not destroying one of one's own. Indeed, killing a demonic being or a bestial creature may even be fulfilling the will of God. Defending the innocent against the predatory machinations of those who are neither human nor humane is clearly noble. It was easy to demonize the yellow Japanese and elongate their teeth into fangs, bow out their legs, and have their lips drip with droplets of blood. It was more difficult to dehumanize the Germans since my mother's family, the Bohns and Bedells, had Germanic roots. Indeed, my Grandmother Bedell had been born in Germany and there was much that I prized in her character and in German cultural achievement.

I was a high school sophomore on December 7, 1941. Warriors underwent a quick metamorphosis:

"dogs" in peacetime, with the outbreak of war soldiers took on the cloak of nobility. Immediately, whatever ambiguity I might have felt about war gave way to clarity and certitude and I began to save my pennies and nickels to buy stamps and pasted them into my war bond books. I had plenty of company as diversity of purpose, personal independence, and egoist autonomy vanished and were replaced by programs for national unity. No worker dared to strike or malinger.

Saving, doing without, stretching things out, repairing, recycling, and "making do" were the values that helped the war effort. Like millions of my peers, I was a happy member of the "clean plate club," since food left on my plate symbolized one of our soldiers going hungry. Those of us who were physically unable to heed our nation's call to arms could nevertheless empathize psychologically with the warrior's privations. It was a glorious time of national oneness.

The desire to join the service was uncontrollable, the mystique and power of the uniform overpowering. I already had experienced the addictive nature of the bonds of sport; intuitively I knew the covenant between warriors was infinitely more cohesive. But I held a secret that filled me with dread of being found "4-F," that is, mentally or physically unfit to serve. That label signified a form of social leprosy, an inner scarlet letter, that could not be exorcised. Neither God nor Father's medical ministrations would be able to remove that mark of the beast. I worried constantly that my secret "thorn in the flesh" might keep me out of the service. No one knew about the limited range of motion of my right knee, for it was a secret I had not even told Father or my best friends. I could not do the squats, the duck-walk, much less the Cossack dance. No matter how hard I tried, a gap of six inches remained between my right heel and buttock. It was a congenital limitation I worked hard to ameliorate. At night I would put hot cloths or a heat pad on my knee. Several times I tied a rope around my thigh and ankle, pulling it tight, and slept all night under this form of torture.

I lived in fear that during a future military physical, a physician would ask me to do the squats, notice my limitation, and send me back home. I would have to endure the accusing stares and silent judgments that demanded to know, "What's wrong with him? He looks all right." I worried about the town gossips: "Neb Benjamin must have a yellow streak down his back."

Those who demonize the military may overlook the deep psychological need for human testing that becoming a warrior can fulfill. In fact, the virtual universality of that need may mean that, as the Bible states, "There shall be war and rumor of war until the end of time." Indeed, aggression, "warism," or violence may be rooted in our genetic inheritance. In any case, it was not war that was enticing to me so much as the testing, the rite of passage. My comfortable middle-class existence had all but eliminated that ritual boundary that normally separates adolescence and manhood. All traditional cultures have highly stylized childhood and adolescent rites of passage that move "mother's boy" to "father's boy" to "one's own man."

In spite of fantasies and tree-top reveries, of drawing my pursuit planes shooting down legions of Japanese planes, of play-acting with my friends at stabbing Germans and bombing their submarines, the masculine reality principle of Father sounded loud and clear:

You are not big, powerful, and supremely competent; instead, you are small, puny, and completely unready. However, matters can change; and if you pay respect to me and my teachings, I will help you escape your impotence and be ready for all life will throw at you.

During my senior year in high school, I looked back at my tender and protected life of 17 years. Like the steps of a one-year-old, my pace was tentative at first; later, the ascent to manhood would demand a stride of Herculean proportions. Thus far I had navigated passages from kitchen chores to garden and yard work to dating and band. From kindergarten through 12th grade, I had marched in lock-step procession, achieved my driver's license on time, hunted many forms of game, become a farm hand, and spent a summer as a railroad "gandy dancer." I had been bloodied in three forms of sport and had tried to be magnanimous in victory and stoical in defeat. My transitions were different than those of my primitive and tribal brothers of ancient epochs, but psychologically they had a common element.

In comparison to youths of earlier times and places, 20th century youngsters experienced rites of passage that were both mild and delayed. Predecessors endured such rituals as facial and body markings, penile sub-incision with cowrie shells, surviving for three weeks alone in the wilderness, publicly reading aloud the day's Torah selection, bringing back a scalp of the enemy, killing wild game with knife or spear. Whatever the rite, its purpose was to prove that its subject would be a contributor, not a liability, to his clan. Deeds were what counted, not promises, intentions, tears, and prayers.

I had endured with some grace the punishment, correction, and discipline that Father, my coaches, teachers, and farm and railroad mentors had meted out during my early passages. I had suffered some deep wounds, but they had scarred over and only I could feel them. I assumed that such wounds were the price that every father's son had to pay. I had earned the right of sonship and apprenticeship, to the end that one day I would inherit accolades, special powers, and knowledge. I was on the way to individuation and separation from

Father and my community-cocoon, just as earlier I had separated from Mother.

To leave home, to become a warrior was the final sign, the final step, of becoming my own man.

Two

The Greatest Disappointment

In early September 1944, approximately a month before my 18th birthday, I took the bus to Minneapolis and entered the United States Navy Air Corps. On earlier visits I had passed the demanding physical and mental tests required to become a naval pilot. My brother, Bob, had preceded me and was now in training. Because of sibling rivalry I longed to surpass him. Thanks to my success in sports, I believed I could. Genetically and environmentally, the dice are loaded in favor of the eldest son, but I was quick and agile although smaller than Bob, and my primary interest in school had been athletics. I had lettered in basketball, football, and track. My room was adorned with medals and ribbons I had won in basketball and in district track contests in the 440 yard run, the pole vault, and the long jump. Put me to the test--I knew I could fly rings around Bob!

After a sleepless night in a small hotel, I joined twelve other anxious and expectant future pilots in the Minneapolis armory. We were called to attention by a swaggering chief petty officer, who then made a shocking announcement. "Listen up! Because hostilities are winding down and your training is long, you probably won't be commissioned before the war ends. The Navy has decided, therefore, to shift you from pilot's training; instead, you'll become air crewmen." I was overwhelmed with disappointment and anger. I would not be able to fly. Fate had turned her back on me. "Damn it," I swore to myself, "I won't become 'an officer and a gentleman.' I'll give salutes rather than receive them. If Father had only signed the papers from the Army Air Corps recruiter who visited our high school six months ago, I'd be at a southern air base flying trainers now."

Nevertheless, I was away from home, in the company of future mates. I would still be in naval aviation, even if my hands would be on machine guns and the radio and radar controls rather than on the pilot's yoke or stick. Moreover, I was making friends. My roommate was Tim Regan of Mankato. His father, a devout Catholic, was an attorney of some stature and was chairman of the Minnesota Democrats for Tom Dewey. Mr. Regan had placed Pat at the Benedictine academy at St. Johns University in Collegeville. He was an intelligent and high-spirited kid who longed for release from his religious prison. Only later did he realize he had simply exchanged one form of servitude for another.

"Shoulders straight, backs against the wall, tuck in your chin, dress right," commanded the chief, "and now we'll see whether you guys have been good little boys. Open your flies and take out your peckers." I was shocked. What did he mean? What was this all about? As I searched for my shriveled genitalia, I saw a navy corpsman shine his flashlight down at the groin of the first man in the row. I was embarrassed to exhibit a precious part of my anatomy in public. I noticed several others surreptitiously taking sidelong glances, evidently estimating how their penises measured up to those of their peers. "Does this mean," I wondered, "that there's a Navy norm down there too?"

"All right men, stretch it out and milk it down. We don't want any of you infected f---ers in this man's Navy." As the corpsman got to me, my pulse rate jumped and my breathing became shallow. He shined his light, looked down, and passed on to the next man. I started breathing again. He was, of course, looking for a discharge that indicated gonorrhea or syphilis. I had just had my first of what were to be many "short arm" inspections. I did not have to ask how the embarrassing ritual got its name. This genital exam was the source of hundreds of jokes for those in the service who regularly endured it.

I don't remember anyone failing the test. I assumed we were a chaste and immaculate group. That opinion would change rather early in my military career.

We marched to the railroad station, boarded the Milwaukee Railroad's famed Hiawatha and roared out of town. In Chicago we transferred to the Illinois Central. After a supper of rice and chicken--it was tough and stringy and not at all like Mother's succulent roasts--I turned in early to my Pullman car berth. The next morning I joined Tim to watch the sun come up. I clocked the speed of the train by watching for the mile posts and found we were rocketing along at 90 miles an hour across the foreign-looking contours of Tennessee. Tim was spinning tales of how he planned to indulge in a surfeit of wine, women and song to make up for time lost during his servitude in the cloistered academy. Already I was homesick for my family, and there was an emptiness in the pit of my stomach that breakfast did not remove.

Three

Boot Camp: A Demanding Discipline

The three months of boot camp are designed to turn the amorphous clay of a civilian into a fire-hardened, finished sailor. Moreover, battles are won by units that have eliminated personal autonomy and eccentricity and whose members move as a homogeneous and monolithic group. "Doing one's own thing" is anathema to the military. Boot camp must destroy particularity by forging a bond among men that makes them willing to suffer, sacrifice and die for each other. Traditional and hierarchic societies, such as Japan, Germany, and China, come by this process far more naturally than cultures, like ours, that have Enlightenment, democratic, and egalitarian roots. This may be the root of why Western societies have always been suspicious of the military and of warrior virtues.

"Boot" comes from the naval term for leggings that are worn during the initiation into the naval fraternity. Like a petitioner for a life of holiness seeking admission as a postulant to a monastic order, we had to be cleansed of all that was profane. The monastic supplicant was stripped, cassocked, and his clothes were thrown over the monastic wall for the beggars. Similarly, I stripped off my clothes. After a 30-second haircut that left my hair less than a quarter-inch long, I was prodded and probed and given a half-dozen shots. Every symbol that marked me as an autonomous civilian--hair, clothes, food, family, friends--was gone.

After being measured in quite cursory fashion, I staggered under the load of Navy garb piling up in my arms. I went in one end of the processing building and, in less than an hour, emerged from the other end a very different being.

As a group, we entered as a motley and polyglot rabble. We exited a bit bewildered with only a small semblance of a Navy corps. It would take weeks of training and indoctrination to make internal what was now only an external reality.

The society I had recently left elevated the individual; here my personal identity was shredded. I had departed from a culture of self-gratification and entered a culture of self-discipline. The hedonistic pastimes of youth--cigarettes, cars, candy, booze, soft drinks, music, sex, girls--were unceremoniously stripped away. In my new reality the group was supreme, pleasure was suspect and sacrifice was good. Boot Camp banished the "I," including even the refuge of identity in one's first name. It took time to learn Navy nomenclature: "Sir, Seaman Benjamin requests permission to make a head call, Sir!"

I cut up my old civilian clothes and flushed them down the toilet. Already I was happy in my new servitude. Amazingly, in my new uniform and enforced conformity, I felt free. Later I would also know that the powerful forces of group socialization can have demonic as well as positive consequences.

After twelve weeks my metamorphosis was complete. On my first liberty in Memphis I experienced Sodom and Gomorrah. It was a stark contrast to the oasis of discipline, respect, and order within the confines of the base. As I walked the streets ablaze with glitter and crowds, my transformation shocked me. Now I saw gluttony, corruption, whores, filth, drunkenness, law-breaking, pornography, sensuality and more. I had become alienated from the very nation that I had pledged to defend, and I was beginning to be contemptuous of

American society. The Navy had transformed me into a military ascetic. I worried that America was becoming a Vanity Fair that was sliding toward the void.

Of the 20,000 men on station, 1,200 made up the "boot camp." I was at the most demanding boot camp in the Navy. My home was in one of the hundreds of two-story wooden barracks that had been hastily constructed after Pearl Harbor. Each measured about 100 feet by 30 feet and housed four platoons of 75 boots. A central aisle separated triple-decker bunks. Bunks were assigned alphabetically, so that all my friends during boot camp had last names beginning with A, B, or C. I was lucky and got a top bunk, six feet above the floor-- too high for my mates to sit on, and warmer in the winter. All my possessions had to fit in a 6' x 1' x 1' metal locker. The floor was fir, glassy-smooth from countless applications of steel wool, soap-stone, and wax by former platoons preparing for weekly inspection. I could have shaved in the reflection. At the end of the barracks was the "head," the naval nomenclature for toilet. (The term came from the projections that overhung the bow of a sailing ship in front of the fo'castle where the sailors slung their hammocks. The ship's company stuck their fannies on these ledges, in which there were holes. Urine and feces thus fell into the ocean and sailors were spared having to empty a commode.) Our toilets and urinals were without partitions and the wooden seats, too, were satiny smooth from being burnished by steel wool. Over the last toilet was a sign: "TO BE USED BY THOSE WHO HAVE VENEREAL DISEASE." A few boots had crabs, and medics shaved their pubic areas and painted them with a purple antiseptic solution. In the shower we treated them like lepers and gave them a lot of space.

I quickly learned a nomenclature that had been handed down from one generation of mariners to the next since the era of tall sailing ships: the landlubber's "floor" is a "deck," whether at sea or on land; likewise, door = hatch; hat = cover; stair = ladder; rope = line; wall = bulkhead; gossip or drinking fountain = scuttlebutt (because that was the site where the daily rumors were heard and told); left and right = port and starboard; ceiling = overhead; 6:30 p.m. = 1830; front and rear = fore and aft; shirt = jumper; kitchen = galley. Throughout history groups, ranging from fraternities to physicians, have coveted the mystique of an esoteric language that differentiates it from the outsider. The purpose, of course, is to indoctrinate new members into a living tradition.

I began a healthy if demanding regimen. The shrill, bugled notes of reveille pierced the air at 5:00 a.m., followed immediately by our drill instructor (D.I.) screaming, *"Hit The Deck, Men!"* A more raunchy cry was, "Drop your cocks and grab your socks!" At the other end of the day, taps was played at 9:30 p.m. The intervening 16-1/2 hours were crammed with marching, eating, cleaning, washing clothes, running obstacle courses, guard duty, class-work, and study. I was eating two to three times as much food as I did at home, and it began to show. I was 5'7" and 134 pounds when sworn in. In six months I grew four inches and gained 30 pounds. (Such stature came too late to pay dividends in high school football and track.) My cardinal complaint was that milk was served only once a day. During the three months of boot camp, I drank only seven glasses of milk. My years of free access to an open refrigerator were gone and with them my consumption of a half-gallon of milk a day. I had left the Land O'Lakes Eden of lush grass, contented Holsteins, and red barns for a southern desert of crabgrass, cockleburs, and cotton. Like my father 30 years earlier on his trip to fight Pancho Villa on the Rio Grande, I surmised that red soil was "not much account" compared to the black gold of Minnesota.

I tried to make coffee taste like cocoa by adding liberal amounts of cream but it did not work.

Because I was good at sports, I enjoyed the rope climbing, hand-to-hand combat, ditch-jumping, wall-scaling, running across logs, hurdling, and other tests of the obstacle course. Speedball, a combination of football and soccer but without padding, was a major sport. I had to throw away all the rules of fairness learned in high school sports. In speedball you could do everything but throw your fists. The toughest drill was to climb a twenty-foot rope using only your hands. Fortunately, my devotion to pole vaulting in high school had developed my upper body strength to a high level. In spite of this, after ascending the rope two or three times, my shoulders and stomach muscles would ache for days. Boot camp sports produced many sprains, lacerations, bruises and broken bones.

Occasionally, a D.I. with sadistic tendencies would put two of us, one a boxer, the other a wrestler, in a boxing ring. He wanted to maximize our "killer instinct" and demanded that all onlookers cheer for their favorite. The wrestler usually won by smashing the boxer off his feet. When I was the boxer, I invariably lost if I could not cold-cock the wrestler as he dove at my feet. The D.I. recited ad nauseam his term--"twisted steel and panther urine"--for the level of fitness he wanted our muscles and spirit to achieve. Smoking took its toll on many of my mates, so I usually was among the top three of our platoon in cross country and obstacle course races.

As required, I signed up for $10,000 term life insurance with my parents as beneficiaries. It was a sum beyond comprehension, and I mused that they would be set for life if I got killed. Deduction of the insurance premium from my pay, plus the deduction for a $25 war bond, left me with net pay of only $29.85 a month. Still, that bought a lot of Coca Cola and gum for those of us who eschewed John Barleycorn and tobacco. Even with my miserly pay, my depression-honed thrift enabled me to save enough to occasionally send a money order to Mother, who converted it to a war bond.

On Monday through Saturday the intense level of activity from 5:00 a.m. to 9:30 p.m. kept us from thinking about home . On Sunday, however, when there wasn't much to do except wash clothes and go to church, homesickness afflicted many recruits; its symptoms were staring off into space and lassitude. As if to provide a remedy, Mother sent me a subscription to *The Pipestone Star*. What I used to deride as "our weekly scandal sheet," I now devoured. I kept up with high school sports and, for the first time in my life, I even read the society and personal columns.

Most of my activities took place within our platoon of 75 men. When we marched, we sang or shouted, in cadence, songs and ditties that usually had raunchy lyrics I have either forgotten or won't repeat. Drill instruction sometimes involved make-believe wooden rifles, and we had 9-, 16-, and 21-count routines that were extremely complicated, especially when marching. We would shift, move our weapons in perfect unison from shoulder to shoulder, rotate them around our waists, touch the buttplates on the tarmac, and slap the tight leather harnesses against the stocks. When our hands hit the leather straps in unison it sounded like a mild explosion. All this we did while dressing right, with our chins tucked in, and staying in step. It was an intricate naval version of patting your head and rubbing your stomach with your hands going in different directions.

The greatest sin a recruit could commit during these exercises was dropping his weapon. Anyone who did this could expect to double-time around the parade ground with the weapon held at arm's length above his head, while shouting, "My rifle is my best friend, and I am a miserable sonofabitch because I abused it! God have mercy on my miserable soul!"

Another cardinal sin was laughing during drill, or giggling, or even uttering a detectable snicker. Those found guilty of such merriment would soon find themselves double-timing around the parade ground, also holding rifles at arm's length above their heads, while shouting at the top of their lungs, "I am a hyena! A hyena is an animal who laughs when there is nothing funny to laugh at! This is the sound a hyena makes! Ha Ha Ha Ha Ha!" Being found culpable of other infractions might result in the guilty party's having to do the duckwalk while holding his rifle horizontally positioned against the back of his neck. The waddler had to shout, "This is the way a duck walks, Quack! Quack! Quack! I will try very hard to walk like a sailor in the future!"

Boot-camp life wasn't all punishment, however. When we performed at near perfection, our voices, weapons, and movement created a form of military harmony that brought a beatific vision to the hard face of our D.I. Sometimes I would wake up at night and hear someone mumbling a cadence:

> Wan-tup-three-fo, threep-fo-you-lef, lef-rye-lef, hada-lef-rye-lef... your lef... your-lef. Dress it up dress it up keep your interval, DRESS IT UP SCUMBAGS. Dig those heels in dig 'em in. Square those pieces away SQUARE 'EM AWAY, GIRLS
>
> Wan-tup-threep-fo.

We memorized dozens of Jody chants such as:

> "I don't know, but I've been told, Eskimo (anatomy) are mighty cold. Give me your lef, your lef, your lef, right lef..."

The marching songs that had been passed down via the Navy's oral tradition helped relieve the boredom and day-to-day sameness of drilling on the tarmac. As we lock-stepped past another platoon, it would answer with the chorus:

> I gotta gal that lives on a hill . . .
> Oh, Little Liza, Little Liza Ja-ane.
> She won't do it but her sister will . . .
> Little Liza Jane.
> Whoa-oh-oh-oh Little Liza, Little Liza Jane
>
> Oh, Little Liza, Little Liza Jane.
> I gotta gal in Lackawanna . . .
> Oh, Little Liza, Little Liza Jane.
> She knows how but she don't wanna . . .
> Little Liza Jane.
> Whoa-oh-oh-oh Little Liza, Little Liza Jane
> Oh, Little Liza, Little Liza Jane.

Because of its exemplary performance, our platoon was chosen to march in the Armistice Day parade in Memphis on November 11, 1944.

Fred Johnson, my DI, was a petty officer, family man, and Navy lifer. His passion was close-order drill. For him it was an art form, and no choreographer could have derived any more satisfaction from staging a ballet than Johnson did from showing us off on the parade deck. For all of his harshness and inner steel, Johnson was a compassionate D.I. He whipped us into machinelike precision, but he also warned us in a paternal manner that we should avoid picking up bad habits in the Navy. "Watch your language. Filthy words do not make you a sailor," he warned. "When you're home on your first leave, you don't want to blurt out in the presence of your family, 'Please pass the f---ing butter.'"

Before taps sounded, we turned to such necessary chores as washing, studying, and writing to our parents and girlfriends. Washing our blue dungarees, whites, and skivvies was an evening ritual. Because of the close quarters that shipboard life entails, the Navy demanded that your body and gear be immaculate. The Navy's first commandment was "cleanliness is next to Godliness" (<u>not</u> "Thou shalt not covet, worship idols, or fornicate"). Having a shoelace out of place could mean a two hour march on the tarmac with a mop over your shoulder. Sometimes we had three inspections a day. Many recruits were "written up" for as little as a barely discernible line of sweat inside their white hats. Sometimes I changed clothes three times a day. For all its strictness, I think it was a good regimen. There are legions of well-groomed men today whose habits of wearing clean, pressed clothes and shined shoes are traceable to the time they spent in the Navy.

For formal inspections we had to place all our gear on top of our bunks. Pillow, leggings, blues, whites, neckerchiefs, skivvies, hats, socks, shoes--everything had to be laid out and placed within a fraction of an inch of where the ideal Naval template said it should be. Since sailing ships were without electricity, protocol forbid ironing. We kept our clothes ship-shape by rolling them tight (much like a jelly roll), inside out, and tying them with short pieces of line. That way they fit compactly into a seabag. It was good discipline for those who had come from chaotic families and environments.

The Navy uniform's blue bell bottoms, with their buttoned, inverted-U trapdoor at the front instead of a buttoned or zippered fly, have been the butt of at least a thousand dirty jokes. Thirteen buttons, symbolic of the original 13 colonies, four on each side and five across the top, had to be undone in order to go to the head. Pity the poor swabbie with a bad case of diarrhea! Anyone caught without all of them buttoned was required to stand on the tarmac for two hours holding a seabag on his shoulder. The Navy, as the most traditional of the services, demanded that its customs be enforced--no matter how inconvenient they might be.

The Navy worried more about the potential contamination of our genitals than our morals. So before we hit Memphis for liberty, we had to watch a film on the use of a rubber. (No one used the term "condom" then.) The scenario portrayed was depressingly conventional: A libidinous sailor from a hick midwestern town has a "wham-bam, thank you, ma'am" encounter with a streetwise hooker. Later he tells a Navy doctor that his urination has become painful and his penis is oozing pus. On being told he has VD, he laments, "But doc, she looked clean!" I was shocked the first time I saw one of these films, whose implication that unmarried sex is ok so long as it's "safe" assaulted my Puritanical conviction that abstinence could be defended on medical, psychological, and moral grounds. I worried that the films of this genre were shown in a snack bar area where women, including teen-age girls, were working. Surely their innocence would be destroyed and their morals corrupted! My Victorian mores were offended that women were exposed to this form of moral contamination. It was tragic, I mused, that the Navy worried more about what our sexual impairment might do to its readiness than about its sailors' moral integrity and the common good.

We were encouraged to attend church on Sunday. The Protestant, Catholic, and Jewish chaplains shared a nondescript chapel where, by turning the altar and removing or adding a few liturgical fixtures, each faith could feel at home in performing its rite. The use of a common facility enforced a form of ecumenism that was unknown among clergy in peacetime. The homilies were

Biblically based, practical guides for those of us preparing for war--honor your conscience, keep your faith, write home, love America, pray for the president and victory, and most importantly, revere your comrades above, on, and under the ocean. Every service ended with singing of the powerful stanzas of the Navy hymn. I was thankful for the years I spent in the Pipestone Methodist choir. I sang with gusto. I pondered the words, especially those of the fourth stanza and whether they would soon have existential meaning for me:

> Eternal Father, strong to save,
> Whose arm hath bound the restless wave,
> Who bidd'st the mighty ocean deep
> Its own appointed limits keep,
> O hear us when we cry to thee
> For those in peril on the sea!
>
> O Christ! whose voice the waters heard
> And hushed their raging at thy word,
> Who walkedst on the foaming deep
> And calm amidst its rage didst sleep.
> O hear us when we cry to thee
> For those in peril on the sea!
>
> Most Holy Spirit! who didst brood
> Upon the chaos dark and rude,
> And bid its angry tumult cease
> And give, for wild confusion, peace.
> O hear us when we cry to thee
> For those in peril on the sea!
>
> Lord, guard and guide the *men who fly*
> Through the great spaces in the sky

Be with them always in the air
In darkening storms or sunlight fair.
O hear us when we lift our prayer
For those in peril in the air!

Outside of Sunday services, I never had contact with a chaplain while in the Navy. Critics have charged that many chaplains were failures as civilian shepherds and, as a result, became hirelings and lackeys of the military. The indictment was a harsh one--that they traded a prophetic calling for the love of a salute, a bit of gold braid, and the status of a uniform. I suspect that the indictment was true in only a few cases. Because chaplains took their orders from line officers, their autonomy was limited by strict boundaries. They had to render more to Caesar than their civilian counterparts. On the other hand, life and death issues are very real in the military, much more so than in the speculative God-talk of academic bull-sessions.

Our chaplains could question neither the necessity of armed combat nor the premise that we were engaged in a "just war," to which the commandment "Thou Shalt Not Kill" did not apply in the usual sense. The Commandment prohibited homicide, not a defensive war that served neighbor love by protecting the innocent. Chaplains could not be pacifists, but had to accept the relative justice of the American cause. Their ministry largely involved a liturgical "mopping up" operation-- bringing God's grace and succor to those facing combat, performing last rites for the dying, writing letters to parents whose sons had been killed, and the like. Some of their civilian counterparts were military-bashers who despised them and mused, "When did you see Christ in khaki?"

But the autonomy of civilian ministers, too, is not without restrictions. The big donors, women's societies, district officers, bishops, and other groups often fashion their own straight-jackets for their clergy. The source of much depression in the clergy may be due to a generalized animus toward parishioners. It is a hatred that many suffer quite subconsciously.

Our D.I. knew we would deal with nonconformists in our own way. Preston Winston was one such nonconformist--a tough and grimy kid from the Bronx. He was losing our platoon points by his attitude, his poorly made bunk, and his dirty clothes. Twice he was the cause of our being routed out of our bunks at 2:00 a.m. for extra marching on the tarmac. We'd had enough; one night six of us carried him into the shower and took a ten inch long brush to him. When the stiff bristles, soaked with bleach, cut into his skin, he quickly lost his New York street toughness.

Everyone had to stand a two hour watch one night a week. Each barrack had a boot who stood fire watch. Hundreds of others were spread across the base in and outside of hangers, the mess hall, class rooms, runways, road intersections, and the like. An outsider couldn't have traveled ten feet without being apprehended. We were being groomed for combat, when such responsibilities are life-and-death issues.

Our classes dealt with the physics of flight, naval air ordinance, hydraulics, mechanics, health and safety, naval regulations, and communication by radio, blinker, and flag semaphore. The latter two forms of transmission were used when radio silence was required, and they were difficult because you had to write without looking at what you were writing. We had to learn the silhouettes and wing spans of 80 planes and 60 ships of both friend and foe. To simulate their movement in and out of cloud formations, images were flashed on the screen for as little as $1/100$ of a second. (An eye blinks at $1/60$ of a second, so it was easy to miss the image.) Wing span memorization was necessary in order to estimate distances for gunnery.

The Navy was an excellent, if limited, pedagogue. It used superb training and memorization techniques. It could indoctrinate, shape, hone, and perfect the latent skills of civilians to serve its needs in an amazingly short period of time. Given its function, the Navy could not offer a liberal arts approach to knowledge. Critical thinking about the classical questions of conflict, the nature of man, the history of empires, and the philosophical issues of peace and war was left untouched.

We also had to pass swimming tests, but they were easy. We practiced the four basic strokes and were tested on whether we could stay afloat for a minimum of five minutes. The requirement was extremely lax considering the fact that, if your plane went down, it might be hours before any rescuers appeared. Lax as it was, initially, over a third of my platoon could not pass the five minute test.

We also acquired a lot of skills a civilian was unlikely to need: we jumped off 50-foot platforms, climbed up and down rope ladders with full packs, and learned how to fashion temporary life jackets out of our dungaree shirts and pants. We learned to increase our chances for survival in burning oil by flailing our hands above the water while still submerged in order to disperse the oil, then making like a porpoise--surface to gulp a breath, resubmerge and swim away from the flaming oil slick, and repeat as often as necessary! It was pretty easy, but of course, it was a dry run. I wondered whether it would really work under burning oil.

I looked forward to a feast on Thanksgiving. The Navy printed a menu that began with cream of celery soup, ended with pumpkin pie, fruit cake and rum raisin ice cream, and included everything in between. It was a public relations piece made to fold, seal and send to the folks back home. My half of a turkey leg was full of pin feathers and wasn't very appetizing. Opposite the bill of fare was a picture of a Captain J.C. Monforty, head of the commissary department, with the essay:

> Good food keeps us in good fighting trim and is therefore a weapon of war. 'Tis said the ingenious Germans can make sawdust fit for human consumption and we know the Japs subsist largely on rice spiced with a bit of dried fish. Well--maybe so, but pause for a moment as you survey your own mess tray heaped with the good things of this bountiful land and thank Almighty God that you are a citizen of that land, privileged to wear its uniform and help keep it inviolate against all its covetous enemies.

Christmas eve 1944 was a poignant time. Instead of being in the bosom of my family, I had guard duty from midnight until 2 a.m. As I marched back and forth across the apron of hangar no. 2, it was cold and a mist filled the air. In the south, a damp cold penetrates to the bones no matter how much clothing you're wearing. Even during deer hunting I had never experienced such a numbing cold.

I thought about opening presents, hanging stockings, the church candlelight service, the Christmas trees inside and outside the house, caroling from door to door, Mother's special foods and preparations, how excited Skippy, our Chesapeake Bay retriever, would be, my sister Mary shaking all the gifts and knowing what each person was getting, the fitful sleep on Christmas eve, getting up at 4 a.m., and much more. My thoughts arched high into the heavens that night and then descended into a frigid little Minnesota town. It was the only Bethlehem I knew. I prayed my family's thoughts arched back to me as I walked my beat on that damp and cold Memphis tarmac. I hoped my parents missed me. I wondered if I would be somewhere with my squadron in the Pacific during the next Christmas.

In spite of such moments, networking of all kinds kept my morale high. I regularly corresponded with a half a dozen of my high school athletic teammates who were in the service. We rejoiced in each other's good fortune and wept at another's grief. I regularly heard from my parents, cousins, aunts and uncles. Some of my tightfisted uncles even enclosed a dollar bill with their Christmas cards. Even the Pipestone Legion sent us a box of candy or a carton of cigarettes.

With the end of our servitude as boots came our first liberty in Memphis; on that occasion my platoon reminded me of Minnesota moose during rutting season. Most boasted of the women they were going to seduce, the liquor they would drink, the girlie shows they would see, the sack time they would enjoy, all the hell-raising they would accomplish. Their first liberty weekend promised to be the military version of a fraternity's *Animal House*.

My mates' fixation on sexual intercourse, real and imagined, was a central ingredient of every conversation. Their view of life was one-dimensional but hardly inaccurate--they were prisoners of their genitalia and women were the keepers of the keys to paradise. The inventiveness of their nomenclature for sex rivaled that of a proper Englishwoman's euphemisms for going to the toilet. While the latter might prudishly comment, "Do you want to spend a penny?" a sailor would boast, "I'm going to get my ashes hauled this week-end!" In my literal-mindedness, I never could fathom what ashes had to do with fornication. I preferred their calling a spade a spade: "I'm going to lift a few skirts this week-end."

A few of my comrades worried about what they believed to be an insidious threat to the strength of their libidos. Rumor had it that, in order to improve its public relations image in Memphis, the Navy had laced our mashed potatoes with saltpeter. The alleged purpose was to reduce the number of Memphis virgins who would be deflowered by the tidal wave of predatory sailors on the weekends. Some of my friends swore they could taste the saltpeter and had not eaten potatoes for weeks.

Sammy, a boot from Chicago, boasted that he had a vial of an exotic potion called Spanish fly that had worked wonders on girls when he was a civilian. He claimed that, after he put a few drops in their drinks, they would be "climbing all over me." Besides finding this obsession with fornication to be simply astounding, I was skeptical about the supposedly magical properties of some ground-up Mediterranean bugs. I had heard the same stories about the properties of Billy goat testicles when I worked on the farm. Some of my mates lost their virginity on their first liberty, not to a Memphis belle, but to a denizen of one of the many Memphis whore houses. They seemed a bit disappointed that the three-minute session didn't give them a bigger kick. They had to pay $10 in advance, which was a lot of money in those days, and there wasn't a refund if you weren't satisfied. Charlie Olson consoled himself by stating that his prostitute told him "Ah can't believe it's y'all's firs' time. Y'all seemed to me like a real pro!" I told him his prostitute wanted him back as a regular customer to take more of his money. For weeks afterwards I kidded him when we were urinating in the head, "Does it burn, Charlie?"

As for myself, the chaste young ladies of Memphis had little to fear from me. My sensual energies were constrained by a Puritanical and Pipestone-fashioned moral straight jacket. Moreover, my feelings regarding women were quite ambivalent. Indeed, the caption under my photo in the 1944 *Pipestone High School Annual* read, "Go Away, Girls." Father's warning--"Neb, if you get married to (i.e., or seduced by) the wrong girl, your future is behind you"--still ricocheted around inside my head. Moreover, I had bonded with men of like values. A former golden glover, Russell Budden, and I sparred in the ring and lifted weights together. Russ was a fitness addict before that became popular. He never drank because, as he stated, "I never want to be out of control."

I always went on liberty with either Budden or someone whose values were cloned from his. On Sundays we sought out a Protestant church and attended divine service. Our motives were not entirely pure. After services, we enjoyed being fought over by families who had sons in the service and wanted to invite us to dinner. We met some wonderful people, ate well, were fussed over, shared pictures and stories, and, not incidentally, saved money. Each family hoped that its act of hospitality would somehow be reciprocated for its son in some distant and unknown home.

Budden also provided me with a pen pal. While I continued to correspond with Ruth Hess, my high school girl friend, he furnished me with the address of a beautiful Croatian girl from Trenton. He spoke highly of her intelligence, her personality, and her Rita Hayworth type curves. We exchanged pictures and I received several boxes of homemade cookies before our correspondence fizzled out after six months.

At the end of the three months of Boot camp, along with one-fourth of my platoon, I tested high enough to begin aviation radioman's training and I moved 1000 feet west across the fence. I started an 800-hour course on Naval radio instruction, of which 200 hours would be devoted to International Morse Code. There was a 40 percent wash-out rate, but I chose radio because of its high expectations and responsibility. Now I could sleep until 6:00 a.m. and the leggings were off for good. The rest of my mates were shipped off to ordnance and mechanics school in Norman, Oklahoma.

Four

Radio and Radar Readiness

On December 26, 1944 I started aviation radio school, an intensive 20-week course. Every day we had three mind-numbing hours of code, but, happily, the excruciating boredom gave way to two hours of trap and skeet shooting, swimming, boxing and other enjoyable activities. Or mostly enjoyable; I had a persistent fear that I would wash out of training because of an inability to hit deflection shots.

Breaking clay pigeons in trap shooting is fairly easy, since "the bird" moves away from you with only a slight deviation to the right or the left. Skeet shooting, on the other hand, is done from one of seven standing positions placed on a large half circle. Clay pigeons were released at a variety of speeds from enclosures at each end of the 180° arc. Each of the seven positions required a different but almost instantaneous calculation by the shooter as to the vertical, horizontal, velocity, and distance components necessary to "powder the bird." Hopefully, the future aerial gunner could deliver his 12-gauge shotgun's load to the exact point where it would intersect with and destroy the curving clay pigeon. I had no basis for contesting the Navy Air Corps dogma that those who were mediocre at skeet would be incompetent airborne gunners, and thus be a hazard to their air crewmen.

My problematic shooting capability had been a problem even at home, where my high school friends Les Kallsen and Bob Alton were "dead-eye Dicks" and much better than I at knocking down pheasants and ducks. I could hit straight-away shots, but those at right angles were difficult. After breaking 10 clay pigeons in a row at trap, I missed the first three at skeet. Fortunately, my instructor was nationally ranked in the sport and knew exactly what my problem was: I was stopping the movement of the shotgun instead of continuing to follow the target as I pulled the trigger. I had to follow through.

The next seven birds shattered. I couldn't believe my eyes! Had I really done that? I was ecstatic and wrote home: "Bring on those pheasants!" I would remain in the program. Weeks later when I was really on, I could break 19 out of 20.

After three weeks every aspiring radio man was issued a yo-yo. Tradition asserted that after three weeks of code you should be batty enough to toss a yo-yo around. Every Saturday there were tests at an ever-accelerating pace on receiving and sending code. I moved from 5, to 10, to 15 words a minute in coded groups of mixed letters and numbers and to 20 words a minute in plain language. Those levels were close to the maximum and are best taken on a typewriter. Military code was any group of five letters or numbers.

I resented having a number of officers in our class. "Do they ever screw around!" I wrote home. "They don't care what kind of grade they get because they are commissioned." Printing in block letters required using backward F's and the number 0 with a slash through it. Anyone who failed a test twice was "sent down" to New Orleans. I feared that possibility like the plague. It meant facing the unknown, enduring a humiliating reduction in status to that of a common seaman, and being separated from trusted companions.

I wrote out a sample message and sent it to my parents:

"VI V V2 - A - 00V2V3 - T - V4 930449 OV1 - W - V5 GR 7   BT 3 JAP BB REPORTED HEADING 14 WEST AR"

Fifty years later I am unable to translate the communication, but the various combinations of words, letters, and numbers indicated call signs of planes, the message's originator, time of transmission, position, etc..

When there was scuttlebutt to send home, I was the dutiful son who mirrored my Father's philosophical conservatism. In my letters I enclosed cartoons attacking socialized medicine and criticizing F.D.R. for taking credit for national and military successes while blaming Congress for his failures. I laughed at satires about Fala, the Roosevelts' dog, having an "A" priority that got three servicemen who "only" had emergency priority bumped from a plane. But my letters seldom mentioned the course of the war or the titanic struggles whose human cost was enormous, such as the Battle of the Bulge and the island-hopping campaigns westward across the Pacific. Was knowledge of these events so common that I did not need to mention them to my parents, or was I so busy in my own world that I missed the larger picture? I don't know.

Despite our regular correspondence, my parents and I longed to see each other. My liberty was every other weekend from 6:00 p.m. on Saturday to 8:00 p.m. on Sunday. Dad and Mom flew down to Memphis to visit me and stayed at the Claridge Hotel on February 10-11, and we were together for about 16 hours. It was their first airplane flight. Mother was stricken with air sickness and the rain delayed their connecting flight to Pensacola to visit Bob. Now, 50 years later, strangely enough, I remember nothing of their visit. My letters are opaque as to my feelings about our reunion and how much their coming meant to me.

The Navy kept up our morale by rotating big-name entertainers around the major bases. I heard Kay Kyser's band and Bob Hope's witticisms. Hope knew how to communicate with servicemen, and his raunchy stories were a great hit. I regularly saw patriotic military films such as "Objective: Burma," "God Is My Co-pilot," "The Fighting Lady," and "Sunday Dinner For a Soldier." Wartime film romance was always tender and chaste. Hollywood accepted censorship rules that never allowed depiction of a couple in bed together. If they were sitting on a mattress, an actor and actress had to have their feet on the floor. A romantic tryst would end with a couple kissing and leaning slightly in the direction of the bed, the lean increasingly toward horizontal as the scene faded out.

I believe no other era in American history created so many wonderful songs and had such fabulous artists as did the years surrounding World War II. On the weekends and at the end of a hard day, I would listen to my favorites. The tunes were silvery and light, the lyrics restrained and innocent. The mood they created was romantic yet chaste, optimistic, hopeful, and expectant.

The venom and nihilism of today's Gangsta Rap, acid rock, and the legions of Janice Joplin-types were unknown then. The performers who captured my heart and soul did not dress like skid-row victims or wear earrings, shoulder-length hair and torn jeans, nor did they engage in a catharsis of hate or do pelvic grinds to simulate sexual intercourse on the stage. The entertainers of the war era had a love affair with America. Their vocation was to firm up the courage of those fighting the forces of tyranny. The individuals and groups we heard didn't act out their animus against life and the "establishment" in their performances. The erotic aspects of life and song were always constrained within acceptable moral channels. Even the songs that were filled with passion seemed in fact to be celebrating a courtly or spiritual love. Longing, wistfulness, homesickness, desire, yearning, hoping, wonder, and tenderness seemed to be present in every song, especially in my favorites:

> "You'll Never Know," Dick Haymes.
> "Chattanooga Choo Choo," Glenn Miller.
> "Don't Fence Me In," Bing Crosby and the Andrews Sisters.
> "I'll Walk Alone," Dinah Shore.
> "There! I've Said It Again," Vaughn Monroe.
> "Till The End of Time," Perry Como.
> "In The Mood," Glenn Miller.
> "Der Fuhrer's Face," Spike Jones.
> "Someone Else Is Taking My Place," Benny Goodman, Peggy Lee.
> "There'll Be Bluebirds Over the White Cliffs of Dover," Kay Kyser.
> "I'll Get By (As Long As I Have You)," Harry James.
> "Sentimental Journey," Les Brown and Doris Day.

Fifty years have come and gone, yet the tunes and lyrics seem as fresh to me as they did when I listened to them on my bunk at 18 years of age. Like my mates, I papered the inside of my locker with cheesecake photos of my favorite female movie stars and singers. The most popular pin-ups were Rita Hayworth, Betty Grable, Jane Russell, Veronica Lake, and Lauren Bacall. The bathing suits of our pin-up dream girls contained at least five times as much fabric as the skimpy bikinis today's women wear without a second thought. The bare-bosomed, crotch-shot pornography of *Playboy* and *Penthouse* simply did not exist. I'm glad it didn't, for such explicit depictions would have deprived me of my wonderful illusions about women, the mystery of "forbidden fruit," the tag under my senior photo in the *Pipestone High School Annual*.

Sometimes I injected a little humor into my letters. "We are now having wrestling, Wezzie," I teased. "It is a lot of fun. But we can't bite, pull hair, scratch, or kick the other guy in the shins like Roger and Martha do. Of course, I *know you* don't do those things." Mother and my sister, Martha, regularly sent me cakes and cookies that would have won blue ribbons at the state fair. I'd barely get them unwrapped before my mates would help me devour them. Amid compliments came questions about Martha's age and whether she was married!

On April 28, 1945, I graduated as an aviation radioman and moved 2000 feet farther west to a "confidential" barrack to undertake the four-week program in aviation radar. I began to feel like an old salt. My dungarees had changed to a light sky-blue hue from their original deep navy blue as a result of many washings. In dress, in mind, and in attitude I was 10,000 fathoms from being a "boot." I wrote Father "please notice that 'something new' has been added. Yes, most of us got S 1/C today." It gave me a bit more status and more pay. No sooner had I completed boot camp than the Navy, expecting the war to last longer than had been estimated, reopened the cadet pilot training program. I desperately wanted to sign up, but that would have required a four-year commitment. I knew the war would be over before then, and that I wanted to attend college. So, I continued on to radar training and lamented the fact that the Navy's faulty prognosis in October had prevented me from flying.

Aviation-borne radar ("radio detection and ranging") was a novelty in 1945, and there were a lot of rumors about its hazards. Scuttlebutt had it that too much exposure could make you sterile, impotent, or worse. Our instructors went to great lengths to set our minds at ease by telling us how horny they were and how many children they had sired. Skeptical, but without any real choice in the matter, we began learning operational radar. Our cathode-ray tubes were only five inches in diameter and quite primitive, and staring at the tiny screen was terribly numbing to my brain and eyes, but I was excited by its theory.

I looked at my tiny screen through a foot-long rubberized cone, the purpose of which was to shut off all external light. Electrical impulses sent from airborne sending units would "bounce back" and show up as points of light or "blips." The position and intensity of the "blips" on the radar grid indicated the size, movement, and distance of naval vessels and aircraft. Unlike today's more sophisticated technology, we had no way to distinguish enemy from friendly forces. Our units were very primitive and sometimes there was so much background "snow" I could imagine I was seeing a Minnesota blizzard.

As I came to the end of almost nine months at Memphis, I worried about my next duty station. "None of them are any good," I mused, "since they are all in the South, but I'll take Jacksonville."

Five

From Shotguns to Machine Guns

At 8:00 p.m. on May 11, 1945 I boarded a troop train for Florida. (The day before I left, I was able to negotiate entrance to my old boot camp to see my high school friend Les Kallsen, who had recently arrived there. From my vantage point of eight months' experience, I felt very superior and gave him some tips on survival.) We had a layover in Birmingham, the Pittsburgh of the South. Dick Davis (a new friend from Pennsylvania) and I walked through the city and agreed it was nothing but a large slum. A large sign over one of the avenues read, "BIRMINGHAM, THE MAGIC CITY." Some magic. The fire and brimstone of the city's open hearth steel mills never went out; they burned like a hell of Biblical proportions. A layer of smog overhung the city and cut visibility to two blocks. The "magic city" was paying a fearsome environmental price for the privilege of fabricating the instruments that won the war.

Gunnery school lasted six weeks and served as the meat between two slices of bread--aviation radio/radar school and flight operations. My instruction began to take on an increasingly serious character. I checked out on parachutes, electrically heated flying suits, pressure chambers, oxygen masks, and exposure to minus 35 temperatures. We reviewed the 30- and 50-caliber machine guns and fired and field-stripped the 20-millimeter canon. Shortly after I arrived, a 20-millimeter blew up and killed an instructor and two students. I thanked God I wasn't on the line that day. We alternated between "shooting" with cameras and with machine guns. On average I would expend thousands of rounds of 30- or 50-caliber ammo a day. Each evening we "belted" by metal linkage the ammo that we shot the following day.

    I learned how to operate the electrical and hydraulic turrets on the B-25 Mitchell, the medium bomber General Doolittle had used during his raid on Tokyo in early 1942. My bravado continued: "Last week 16 out of 25 who went up for gunnery got air sick," I wrote home. "This kid doesn't get sick." I added a postscript: "Dad, if you want to go deer hunting and need some 30 cal. shells, let me know." I began earning my "flight skins"--by flying a minimum of four hours a month I received an extra 33 dollars pay a month.

    I enjoyed climbing into a Bendix turret on top of a fire-ranger type tower 100 feet above the ground. Armed with a 12-caliber shotgun, I could rotate the turret 360 degrees and powder the clay pigeons that came at me from all directions. The purpose was to replicate the pursuit or parabolic curve that an enemy fighter would take in an attack on a patrol bomber. Finally, my high school geometry was paying off! When I was "hot," the distance and deflection calculations became automatic and the clay pigeons disappeared in clouds of dust.

    In spite of the roaches, mosquitoes, and bedbugs, Yellow Water, the name of my training camp near Jacksonville, was a sun-drenched heaven compared to the damp and rainy Memphis. The name probably came from the stagnate water and cases of Yellow Fever and jaundice that its location created. I quickly picked up a tan at the Olympic-sized pools on the base. I joined my unit's diving team and was intent on learning new dives. "Have learned two more dives since I've been here," I wrote Mother. "A one-and-a-half and a full back flip from a handstand, both off the high board."

Bob and I met for liberty at Daytona Beach on the first week-end in June. It was good to see him, and to catch up on what was happening in our separate lives. In public and in uniform, however, since he was an ensign and I was enlisted, I felt uneasy. Military tradition demands that officers and rated seamen not fraternize, because doing so would erode the command structure. Egalitarianism is fine in theory, but military discipline is not based on democratic processes, nor are wars successfully fought using them. "Familiarity," as the saying goes, "breeds contempt." There are some human endeavors where caste is required.

As a new gentleman, compliments of the U.S. Congress, Bob seemed to enjoy receiving and returning salutes from the enlisted men. Such symbols of respect, however, fell off markedly when I was with him, because sailors were confused as to what to do. Whether they saluted or not, they were half wrong, because in our duo they had encountered a military hybrid.

Bob, however, seemed hardly to notice either my uneasiness or the sailors' confusion; in fact, he could talk of nothing but romance. He had fallen hard for two southern belles, Betty and Marian, who were identical twins. He had discovered this double bounty at a strict Methodist Florida college. I could not begin to describe his flights of ecstasy regarding their beauty, personality, intelligence, charm, and, of course, their physical dimensions. He was transfixed, moon-struck, and pole-axed by the southern incarnation of the Wrigley's Spearmint Gum jingle: "Double Your Pleasure, Double Your Fun." I warned him of the alleged vices of southern women, however nicely and deceptively they might be packaged. "Remember," I warned, "they lack the substance and the no-nonsense homemaking and motherhood qualities of northern women. If you don't believe me go see *Gone With The Wind* again." Our indoctrination as adolescents had led us to believe Minnesota produced the best corn, fish, hogs, butter, cheese, and women in the world, although not necessarily in that order. I enjoyed kidding my brother over his plethora-of-women problems and wrote home and told my parents to do the same.

But Bob needed help. He wanted to know which one to choose. He admitted that the present course was expensive and that his last dinner date with Marian had greatly diminished his bank roll. I never knew how the agonizing choice between two beauties of the post-bellum South was resolved. Perhaps a new duty station assignment absolved him from having to make an agonizing selection. Later, after receiving the following letter in which he described his fantasies of post-war college life, I wondered whether his mind had been damaged by engine fumes, hominy grits, or southern cat fever:

> You know, when we go to school after the war we'll really do things up brown. I can see it now: we'll have a suite of three rooms: one room (the sleeping room) will have two beds with innerspring mattresses, two dressers, large closet, etc. The next room will be strictly for study purposes. In it we'll have lots of bookshelves and nice study desks with good lamps over them (we <u>will</u> be studying now and then you know). The next room will be to entertain our friends (strictly for bull sessions). We'll have a radio (which we can plug in in our bedroom also) and an icebox to keep milk, orange juice, etc., in.
>
> Out front we'll have a roadster (top down, of course) and though about 15 other guys will probably own it with us, we'll still get to use it now and then. After breakfast, (out of our

icebox) you can go over to play basketball and flirt with the coeds, and I'll go over to the "U" to see if I can't pound a little knowledge into my head. At night I'll come back without the knowledge, but you'll probably have two or three coeds, so that will make up for my lack of success. We'll all pile in the roadster; the top will be down, we'll all be yelling, and we'll end the day with a big spree (which you will pay for with the money you saved, and I <u>didn't</u> save, while in the Navy). How's it sound? Need any improvements--more rooms, less rooms, more women, less women? You name it, <u>we</u> got it. Your brother, Bob.

I sent his letter home with a note scratched on the side: "Isn't this a masterpiece? I agree with Bob's super-duper plan. Dad, how about you?" On June 17 I sent a Western Union telegram, "Father's Day Greetings to the best dad in the world."

In early June I applied for a new PB4Y-2 squadron that was being formed. The Navy acronym meant: PB = patrol bomber, 4 = fourth major design change, Y = Convair-Consolidated/San Diego (manufacturer's symbol), 2 = second minor design change. Bob had wanted to fly this navy modification of the B-24 Liberator but humored me: "Well, kid, sure hate to see you get 'Ys,' but when you're shot down, don't worry: we'll come along in our 'old reliable' PBM (patrol bomber, Martin aircraft corporation) and pick you up."

As I continued my gunnery training, I began to experience a wonder and fascination at the military's unique sights and sounds. From 10,000 feet in the air the world looks beautiful beyond describing. I was entranced by the beauty of the verdant land and trees, the many shades of blue and violet in the ocean, and the clouds that were ever-changing into an infinity of different forms. I also began to learn more about air combat. We would dive down at a 45-degree angle, drop some flares on the water and fire our 50-caliber weapons. With cameras instead of machine guns we would "shoot" Hellcats as they flew pursuit curves. We dropped make-believe bombs on tethered ocean rafts and on uninhabited islands. Other planes pulled sleeves that we fired at using color coded rounds to help determine who had the highest score.

On July 5 Western Union delivered the following message to my parents: "15 days delayed orders; home approximately 10th." After nine months I had my first leave! Without priority or emergency leave it was impossible to fly, so I took the Dixie Flyer to Chicago and then caught the Milwaukee Hiawatha to Sioux Falls, South Dakota, where my parents picked me up. Because of the congested and frenetic transportation, some of my friends were able to spend only three days of their leave at home. My family was overjoyed to see me and on Sunday they hosted a reunion with my Hutchinson uncles and aunts. After church, Mother had a picnic dinner in our back yard. Afterwards, she and my grandparents left for Kee Nee Moo Sha, our traditional vacation spot, to help restore the camp to some semblance of order. Granddad wanted to fence in the abandoned resort, which Father had bought for back taxes, and run some sheep and goats on the land to beat back the foliage.

Six

Preparing for Combat

I checked into my fifth duty station, Jacksonville Naval Air Station, in July of 1945 for eight weeks of operations. It was a polyglot base with army, navy, and civilian air facilities. There were Avengers, Hellcats, Wildcats, Flying Fortresses, TBM's, PBY's, and much more. I went out and looked at my plane, the PB4Y-2, the Privateer, and liked what I saw. The Privateer was a naval modification of the famous B-24 Liberator.

The plane's specifications were awesome. It had a wingspan of ll0 feet, a length of 75 feet, and four Pratt & Whitney air-cooled engines, each rated at 1350 horsepower. Fully armed and loaded, the Privateer weighed 62,000 pounds, had a maximum speed of 245 mph at 13,750 feet, a range of 2,630 miles, and carried a crew of eleven. Its service ceiling was low, 21,200 feet, because the Navy wanted it to bomb accurately. In my innocence I believed it to be the most beautiful and powerful plane in the world, one that would keep me safe as we wreaked havoc on the demonic Japanese Empire.

The Privateer had several distinguishing features. A single-29 foot vertical tail took the place of the Liberator's twin tail and made for a very stable aircraft. It carried six hydraulically or electrically operated twin 50-caliber turrets. One spine-mounted dorsal Martin A-3 turret was situated immediately behind the cockpit, the other just ahead of the vertical stabilizer. Interrupters prevented a gunner from shooting off the tail of his plane. The two waist blisters could deflect down ten degrees below vertical (the guns' field of fire converged 30 feet below the plane) so that no additional belly defensive armament was required. An Erico ball turret at the front of the plane was complemented by a Consolidated A6B turret in the tail.

We were a veritable flying porcupine of defensive power. If given voice, our 12 50-calibers would shout, "Jap Zeros, keep your distance!" We could throw off infinitely more deadly quills than any lumbering porcupine.

The plane had a seven foot extension added to the forward fuselage to accommodate a flight engineer's station. Rounding out the Privateer's defenses were a half-dozen radar and astro blisters whose purpose was to shoot the stars. With all that radar and radio technology to keep track of, I began to realize why the performance tests on radio and radar had been so tough. In all, 739 Privateers were built and several remained in service up until 1964.

I felt like a cocooned chrysalis in my rear turret. Had I been any taller or heavier I would not have been assigned that responsibility. I assumed a semi-fetal position after shoe-horning myself into it through the 20-inch by 18-inch door. I moved the turret and guns up and down, port and starboard, by means of a handle-bar yoke on which the firing button was located. My only passive defense was a 3-foot by 2-foot curved plate of laminated glass, 3-inches thick, through which I viewed my constricted world. More worrisome was the fact that the severe limitation of space did not allow wearing a parachute. We were supposed to wear our harnesses at all times. In the event that "May Day" was called, I was supposed to clip on a chest pack from the main cabin. The problems with that plan were many. The parachutes were kicked around and never stowed properly. My turret was the most difficult to exit. Therefore, I would be the last in line in securing a chute. I envisaged a battle royal over them if we ever had to abandon the aircraft. Heroism sounds great in July 4th speeches, but I wondered whether the fraternal bonds of my crew would hold up in a crisis. I did not as yet view them as a substitute family equal in value with my kith and kin.

Moreover, the clip-on chutes were only 16 feet in diameter, whereas a regular chute is 20 feet. I would come down at an excessive speed and, if I landed on land, might break my legs or worse. If there wasn't time to exit the turret when the plane was going down, I could rotate to 90 degrees, push myself out and do a free fall, though, of course, I would have no chute. During rare moments of lucidity, I silently cursed the engineers who had designed the contraption. Their Lilliputian brains had made the turret for midgets. But I was young and unbloodied, so most of the time I believed I was immortal. Nevertheless, I hoped the Almighty heard my silent prayers that I would never have occasion to need a chute.

I joined a plane crew that had been formed four weeks earlier and whose radioman/tail gunner had been called back for flight training. Because I had not been a part of the initial bonding process, I came in as an alien. The crew scrutinized my radio, radar and gunnery expertise. They took a wait-and-see attitude, but in the days that followed, my competence in gunnery and radio led them to accept me. Except for the three officers, the eight members of our flight crew bunked together. Our rooms were in a tarpaper shack that had been hastily constructed a few years earlier.

A photo taken in front of our aircraft shows the crew of my eleven-member Privateer family and includes comments I wrote about each: John Gorbold, Aviation Ordinanceman 3/c, 18, has been in the Navy 13 months, Detroit, Michigan, "a swell guy"; Russell Budden, Aviation Radioman, 3/c, 18, has been in the Navy 21 months, Trenton, N.J., "I pal around with him the most"; Kenneth Gibson, AOM 3/c, in 13 months, "a farm boy from Kansas, not the brightest guy in the world"; Philip Smith, ARM 3/c, in 3 years, Trenton, N.J. "only 5'4" tall"; Harvey Crawly, Aviation Machinist mate 3/c, in 2 years, "a good Yankee from the northern tip of Maine, wonderful skater, a good guy"; William Lawson, AOM 2/c, 20, in 1-1/2 years, "the playboy of the crew and the bombardier"; William Marr, AOM 3/c, in 2-1/2 years, "the clown of the crew"; Robert Coverdell, AMM 1/c, in 5 years, from Utah, "our super-deluxe plane captain, knows the PB4Y-2 backwards and forwards." I listed the officer's names but not their home towns or interests. They were a breed apart and, even if regulations permitted it, we did not want to fraternize with them.

Our flights were long and tiring. My first was a radar-directed night bombing run down to Lake George in southern Florida. Our number 4 engine started torching soon after take-off and flames were shooting out 100 feet behind the engine. Unlike civilian aircraft, military planes were stripped to maximize the amount of ordnance and fuel they could carry. Sound-deadening materials, upholstered chairs, and other creature comforts were absent. The constant whine of four screaming engines, vibration of the airframe, wind streaming through gaps in the bomb bay doors, metal stresses, and atmospheric changes, all these and more quickly sapped our energy level. Our toilet was a "piss tube," a funnel arrangement with a plastic tube that carried urine outside the plane. Ten-hour navigation flights over Bermuda and other Caribbean Islands were the most arduous. However beautiful the Privateer, and in spite of my good physical shape, the plane was a man-killer. The fatigue that set in on completion of these ordeals left me feeling like a limp dish-rag, and sleep overtook me the instant my body touched my bunk.

One night I came down with a vicious and debilitating illness. Whatever its medical nomenclature (I doubt that the doctors knew what it was), we called it swamp or cat fever. My symptoms were a high fever and aching muscles and joints. It struck late one night and I had to walk to sick bay. On the way I collapsed and briefly passed out. Fortunately, I was on the grass and wasn't hurt. When I came to, I walked a block, sat down and put my head between my knees for several minutes and then continued on, repeating the process all the way to the infirmary. It took me an hour to go a mile. My temperature registered 105.5 degrees when I staggered in. The shame of it all, I mused. The shame of it all--I would die in sick bay rather than as a hero in the Pacific!

In spite of Father's indictment of government and socialized medicine, I was treated kindly. I was given some shots, and a Navy nurse brought a fan. Periodically she changed the cold wet cloths that helped reduce my fever. She stayed most of the night and brought me ice cream. I was in for five days.

A few days before my illness, I had lost my wallet and I.D. card and had to wire home for some money. For the carelessness of losing my I.D., I had to stand a Captain's Mast, a minor court marshall, and was restricted to base for two weeks. My experience at Jacksonville was not a happy one.

In a late July letter I made one of my few references to the wider war: "The war situation is beginning to look up. I can't see how Japan can expect to come out on top when it's fighting the U.S., Great

Britain, Russia and China." It was barely two weeks before Hiroshima. On the afternoon of August 12, we were circling Jacksonville waiting for radio permission to land when suddenly, I saw Roman candles and rockets exploding against a backdrop of dark thunderheads. I tuned our radio to a civilian station and picked up the news that Japan had capitulated. I shouted over the intercom, "The war is over! The war is over! The Japs have given up!"

Within days, my squadron completed operations and I caught the Dixie Flier for three weeks' leave. I was to rejoin my squadron at Camp Kearney, California, on September 8, 1945. I had a wonderful time at home. I brought the news that I had been promoted to aviation radioman second class--the equivalent of a buck sergeant in the army--and Mother sewed my new stripes on my uniform. Next she ordered me to go down to Songes Photography, where I sat for the only formal picture taken of me during the time I was in the Navy. I also visited the old haunts of my high school years. In church I was all seriousness. Head erect and my back like a plumb-line, I was ever-conscious that the congregation would judge the Navy through my behavior and manner. Later, walking through the court house, I felt honored at seeing my name among the hundreds from Pipestone county who were serving their country. Most home windows displayed little flags with red stars indicating how many family members were in the service. I felt sorry for those whose flag showed a gold star; it meant a son had been killed in action.

Ruthie Hess and I saw a lot of each other and stayed out fairly late several nights. The result was an enforced chat with Father on the way to a house call at a farm. He reminded me that some girls use their physical charms to seduce their boy-friends in order to get pregnant. "Oh No!," I inwardly remonstrated, "not my delectable but chaste little Ruthie?" But I did not have his wealth of experience to dispute his empirical evidence. As a country physician he certainly knew more than I did about "fast" girls, sexual confessions, backseat liaisons, and babies that needed only five months gestation after a quick trip to the altar.

Father had a Hobbesian rather than a sentimental view of human nature. I convinced him that his cynical generalization about women did not apply to Ruth Hess. I surmised that his lecture may have had a covert purpose, that of finding out whether Ruthie and I had "gone all the way." I assured him that my virtue was intact, that I was prudent and wary and had adopted a modicum of his suspicion of the fairer sex. He knew I was not ready to get serious with any girl, no matter how talented, beautiful, virtuous or aggressive. Father needed reassurance that a goodly portion of his puritan ethic, along with his genes, had been successfully transferred to his second-born. He admitted he had been negligent and could have taught me much more about sex. I replied that I had done a pretty good job of picking up most of it on my own. He seemed relieved and we both relaxed as our conversation shifted to damning Roosevelt and the democrats.

Seven

Military Melancholy

On September 8, 1945, as ordered, I rejoined my squadron at Camp Kearney, located 16 miles north of San Diego. I had puddle-jumped from Sioux Falls to get there, making seven landings and take-offs on a civilian DC-3. Air travel was Spartan. Kool-Aid and hard candy were the only sustenance dispensed by cabin attendants. The transition from Florida's verdant landscape to the desert gravel of California shocked me. "The people around here would starve if it weren't for the Midwest," I wrote, forgetting about the Imperial valley. The only beauty I saw was a mountain range northeast of our base.

The cessation of hostilities with Japan brought about powerful centrifugal forces throughout the armed services. Everyone was hell-bent to get out, and I was no exception. (I knew the adage concerning the warrior: "heroes in war, dogs in peacetime.") Discharge was based on a point system and points were in turn based on one's number of months in the service. Everyone eagerly counted up his points. Already we were a crew without officers, since our pilot, co-pilot, and navigator were in the process of being discharged. Each issue of *The Pipestone Star* listed the names of those who had already returned to civilian life. Depressed and embittered, I wrote home, "It will be a heck of a long time before Bob and I are out; I have only 15 points and he has 23."

Meanwhile, protocol continued as if the war were still on. We took courses in jungle survival, honed our gunnery skills, checked out our swimming fitness, and had more typhoid and tetanus shots.

And we continued to write and receive letters. I had a Fleet Post Office ("F.P.O.") address that detoured my mail through San Francisco, indicative that our squadron could be sent to the Pacific. (F.P.O. was the military equivalent of "general delivery," the purpose of which was to protect the secrecy of specific units in the theater of war.) With a 50 per cent bonus for flying and 20 per cent for overseas pay, I was making $140 a month. I was figuratively rolling in wealth and sending a $100 money order home each month. Many letters to Mother contained the Johnny-one-note query: "P.S. Have you received my money order? Please buy a bond with it."

As October and autumn arrived, activity decreased. We mustered in twice a day and followed the shade around the barracks as we played cards. I worked out with the punching bag, went swimming, and played basketball and tennis to reduce the boredom as I waited for the Navy to decide what to do with our squadron. As the season progressed, our tar-paper shacks provided little protection against the desert cold at night. I would wake up shivering and hear the plaintive call of the coyotes.

Most week-ends I would stay at the YMCA with members of my crew, attend a football game, go roller skating, go to church, and return to base Sunday night. Sometimes I would rotate around the immediate camps-- Elliot, Miramar, Pendleton--to see friends from Pipestone and from previous duty stations.

Occasional opportunities to share liberty with members of the Benjamin tribe were especially enjoyable. Uncle Mac, a major in the Army Medical Corps, was stationed at the Mitchell Convalescent hospital at Camp Lockett, which was less than a mile from the Mexican border. We spent many week-ends together playing golf and tennis, riding cavalry ponies, and going to church. Mac's oldest son, Mac Jr., had just graduated from boot camp at Camp Elliot, and he and I often went to the beach together. Uncle Mac had a terrific personality and was my favorite uncle. He had been an ambulance driver in World War I and had witnessed the terrible carnage of trench warfare. "Neb, the emasculation of the military after 1918 helped bring on World War II," he warned. "I understand the pell-mell rush into civilian life, but it will have tragic consequences if we commit the same mistake now."

Father said Mac had gone to Marquette, an "inferior" medical school. But acting under the constraints of *noblesse oblige* and the loyalty demanded of their common Benjamin blood and genes, Father helped Mac set up practice at Jasper, 11 miles from Pipestone. Father's largess, however, was doomed to failure. "Mac--Neb take note--married the *wrong* woman." Wife Virginia, R.N. a striking southern belle from Virginia, had "gotten her hooks into Mac" and spent his money as if it grew on magnolia trees. "All of my children reflected the hard times of the Depression," Mother reminisced, "and wore clean but patched and faded hand-me-downs. Virginia's three youngsters were always dressed in expensive pinafores and sailor suits."

Mac was not without faults of his own, including what some considered to be rather modest medical skills. For example, in a home-confinement case, he lost the diminutive wife of Olaf Knudson, a farmer of Paul Bunyanesque physical stature. "I told him to take his wife to the hospital," Mac told me, "that with his size, his baby would 'split her apart'." "No way; I vas born in dat bed," remonstrated Olaf. "Vat ist gut enuf for me, ist gut enuf for da missus unt my kid." After Mrs. Knudson died in childbirth, a lawsuit followed and, although Mac won, his reputation was in the gutter. After the trial he took his healing skills to the less litigious arena of the

Civilian Conservation Corps for a time before entering the army.

But Mac seemed fated to live under a medical nemesis. After extensive training in tropical diseases in Panama, the army sent him to New Guinea. He promptly came down with malaria, jungle rot and a few other exotic diseases, the very ones he was supposed to treat. Airlifted home for R & R, he discovered wife Virginia had turned his children against him. Harsh words followed and Mac exited lest the argument escalate to blows. Reluctantly, he then committed the blackest of all sins among the puritanical Benjamin tribal prohibitions-- he got a *divorce*! Surprisingly, the tribe was compassionate and forgiving. Everyone knew Mac had been blind-sided by a "sweet-talking, southern Jezebel."

Mother's parents, Granddad and Grandma Bedell, usually wintered in Long Beach. True to their Depression-spawned values, they would hunker down for winter in a miserable but cheap two-room apartment. (Like other Midwest "snowbirds," they checked the daily weather reports and took sadistic pleasure whenever an Alberta clipper swept over the Midwest.)

One Saturday I hitch-hiked up to Long Beach and found my grandparents in bed at 8 p.m. I rousted them out because I wasn't going to sleep in the hall. The next day Granddad took me exploring. His major activity was attending the "University by the Sea," better known as the "Spit and Argue Club" on the Long Beach municipal pier. It was the California version of Speaker's Corner in London's Hyde Park, only a bit more violent. Disciples of Amy Semple MacPherson attempting to save lost souls competed with atheists shouting that the churches only wanted people's money. Everyone had a recipe for heaven on earth. Whether capitalists, communists, socialists, free-lovers, millionaires, ex-nuns, bums, hookers, Moral Rearmament advocates, "fundies" of the left or right--all were fanatics with a gift of gab. It was a three-ring circus without an admission charge. Fights often broke out, and Granddad said he had seen as many as eight squad cars there at once. I tried to provoke him into mounting his own soap box to become a "professor for a day." I suggested a few possible lecture titles: "The American Trinity: God, Old Glory, and Iowa Land"; "My Story: Pennsylvania to Iowa With $20"; "The Recipe for Growing One-Pound Tomatoes"; and "How To Buy Iowa Land and Become Rich." But he was a man of innate shyness, albeit with a reservoir of quiet dignity. He didn't take up my challenge.

Back at the base, I worried about my future. Each week a number of crews flew to Navy bases in the Pacific. Scuttlebutt had it that we would get a set of new officers and be sent to Alaska for six months. Given the Privateer's low service ceiling, the certainty of wing ice, the fog, the mountains, and our primitive radar, the Alaska theater was the epitome of hazardous flying. Besides, up in Seward's "ice box" I would be "out of sight and out of mind" and could not massage my points for an early discharge.

Still, the number of Privateers on the tarmac remained at about 100. Crews were being dismembered so rapidly that only 10 percent of us were flying. Members of my crew with enough points were being rotated out so that by November 1, only five of us were left. Rumors surfaced that if we went to the Pacific, we wouldn't be back for two years. "Guys like you with 16 points don't stay stateside," an aircrew chief pontificated. On some of the envelopes I sent home I drew the omnipresent "Killroy Was Here" cartoon with the caption: "Where Dat Discharge?" With the scarcity of news, I had to use jokes in my letters, always clean ones, as filler: "A wolf is a creature of the male species who has devoted the best <u>leers</u> of his life to women."

On November 8 the Navy made a decision to allow the members of our pilotless crew to apply for Shore Patrolman school in our home naval district. After a physical and interviews, I was accepted along with Budden and Gibson. We were elated; scuttlebutt had it that one might be able to pull a few strings in one's home naval district and be discharged earlier. Moreover, I read of gangs in Hawaii and elsewhere "rolling" servicemen. I even felt a subtle shift in sentiment toward the military in California--heroes in wartime, dogs in peacetime. "It's about time the servicemen stand up for themselves," I wrote home. "I never walk down a dark street alone but always with one or two of my crewmates so some civilian won't bop us over the head, beat us up, and take our money." People had short memories, and now some people considered those in uniform to be bums. I began to wear civilian clothes on liberty.

I spent a week at Coronado Heights, where our barracks were only 600 feet from the ocean. One day Budden and I ran down the beach and stumbled into an abandoned battery of 155mm, Long Tom artillery rifles, plus range finders and machine gun nests. Tunnels led to underground bunks and mess halls. We were in a restricted area that had been hastily constructed in 1942 when there was fear of a Japanese invasion. Those were days of panic, when honorable and patriotic Japanese-Americans from our three western states were moved into "relocation" camps and fortifications were thrown up for a threat that proved to be non-existent.

On November 23, 1945 the day after Thanksgiving, I left by train for what proved to be my final duty station. I was depressed, believing that a year hence I would probably be spending another Thanksgiving in the Navy. Compared to the daily torrent of men the Army was discharging, the conservative Navy release rate was a mere trickle.

Eight

Radioman to Rails

Chicago's Tower Hall, a Navy-commandeered hotel, was a serviceman's dream. Seventeen stories high and only two blocks from Lake Michigan, it had automatic washing machines, a swimming pool and civilians who both cooked and served the chow. It was the Navy version of the Ritz, and I slept between two white sheets for the first time in the service. Outside our door was a monument to the first Chicago water tower and a plaque signifying the site where Mrs. O'Leary's cow kicked over the lantern that started the conflagration of Chicago.

As neophyte shore patrolmen, we replaced professional SPs who had been civilian policemen and railroad detectives in civilian life. I heard many macabre stories of how they man-handled drunken or disobedient naval personnel. I surmised that their tales had been embellished to have the desired effect on us. I knew my parents worried about my becoming a Navy cop. I assured them that at 175 pounds on a 5'11" frame with hardly an ounce of fat, I was adequate to the task. Like Catholic nuns and Mormon missionaries, SPs were always paired and I assured them that I would try and pick a partner who was a "big bruiser."

Our formal instructors were former lieutenants and captains from city police departments. Our course of study involved a variety of firearms--the .45-caliber Colt automatic, the .38-caliber Colt special revolver, and the Browning submachine gun. We took lessons in karate, jujitsu, and other forms of hand-to-hand combat. Lectures dealt with topics such as civil commotion, interrogation, preserving evidence, the handling of officers and service women, guarding prisoners, Navy law, reasonable force in making arrests, train riding, and the right and power to enter private homes.

I passed the theory part of the course with a 4.0, and then was paired off with a seasoned SP for some roving patrols. (I would have preferred going by Jeep rather than on foot.) For three weeks I was an apprentice of Mike Prescott, a former railroad detective from Nashville. Mike was a great mentor and I absorbed everything he taught me about self-protection and avoiding dangerous situations. Later, when I was on my own, I inwardly thanked him a dozen times for teaching me how to preserve myself from harm.

We surveyed train stations, patrolled the loop, wandered in and out of bars, alleys, and flop houses, and made some quick train trips to Cincinnati, Cleveland and Pittsburgh. I put in for Minneapolis for detachment duty, but I had to admit that Chicago treated its servicemen well. Opera and theater tickets were free, as were the street cars. It would be hard to leave.

Because of my test scores, I was selected for "carrier duty," e.g., riding trains. The Navy picked those at the top of the class for trains because there was no back-up available. If you had 1500 men on a train, each with a bottle and hatred for authority, all hell could break loose. An SP would have a hard time calling for reinforcements from the Great Northern train #315 somewhere in the middle of Montana. My tongue and bearing would have to be as important as my physical strength. For the next seven months, my letters bore

One evening in December I went roller skating with Kenneth Gibson. He asked a girl to skate with him and soon they were paired off. The problem was, she had come with another girl. "I can fix that," Kenny told his new friend. "Benji is a crew member friend of mine. He'll get along fine with her." That was my introduction to Jeanne Walker, a girl from the Irving Park section of north Chicago. Jeanne was a 5'7" brunette with long wavy hair who was executive secretary to a bank vice president. A bit on the thin side by my standards, Jeanne more than made up for it with a charming personality and an infectious laugh. I dated her seriously for the next seven months and the Walker address became my home-away-from home during that time. On December 17 I wrote to my parents:

> I don't think I've told you but I'm going with a swell girl by the name of Jeanne Walker. She's a nicer-looking girl than Bob could ever go out with. Also, she's a Methodist, so you see I don't have to go to the Baptist church like somebody I know.

On Christmas Jeanne felt sorry for me and invited me to her home for dinner. I wrote that her mother was sick "but that Jeanne had cooked a fantastic repast." Within days I received a letter from Father asking whether Mrs. Walker was a "chronic invalid." Father saw everything through a medical prism. He didn't want any son of his to get serious with a girl whose genetic lines were sullied. He assumed, of course, that the Benjamin pedigree was immaculate.

In a preemptive strike, I answered a battery of questions that I knew were on the minds of my parents. By nature they were suspicious and judgmental and I had to allay their fears. "The Walkers are a fine *Methodist* middle class family . . . they have *high morals* . . . they have treated me *very well* . . . they have *three children* . . . Mrs. Walker is an *excellent* homemaker . . . I think they are a *very wholesome* family . . . Mr. Walker comes from *Iowa*, and went to *Iowa Wesleyan College* . . . he is an insurance investigator . . . they *don't drink*." Whatever the prevailing thought might be regarding the classic nurture v. nature controversy, Father always sided with ancestry as the most important determinant of character. I tried to moderate my parent's critical judgments by sending her picture home: "Even your critical eye, Dad, should tell you that Jeanne is not the homeliest girl in Chicago." I didn't mention that Mr. Walker was a chain smoker and had a persistent hack.

My "carrier duty" alternated among the three major northern routes to the west: The Northern Pacific to Mandan or Bismarck; The Chicago, Milwaukee, St. Paul & Pacific to Miles City; The Great Northern to Havre. The Great Northern had oil-burning diesel engines, while the Northern Pacific and Milwaukee still burned coal. After a round trip on either of the latter two lines, my hair and clothes were powdered with a fine layer of coal dust.

At each western terminus, a Shore Patrolman from the Seattle Naval District would take control of the train; then I always had a 24-hour layover before heading back to Chicago. I was able to save 50 percent of my per diem allowance. My hotel allowance was $2.00 a night but I never paid more than $1.00. Montana was cattle country, and I could get a 12-inch by 6-inch steak for 50 cents even though my meal allowance was a generous $1.00. 1946 was B.C.--before cholesterol, and I ate for enjoyment, not to escape a nursing home. I wish I had saved a fraction of the silver dollars that passed through my hands. On the return ride, I always had a free berth in the Pullman car and all the food I wanted in the dining car.

I enjoyed the west and the railroad fraternity. The openness and beauty of the big sky country, tight jeans, cowboy boots, slot machines, inexpensive food, and the ranchers' friendliness, self-reliance and individualistic assertions of freedom made a deep impression on me. I am not at all surprised that a deep and abiding resentment against an ever-expanding and omnipotent state would take root and flourish in such soil.

I became a close friend of two conductors, and they had me to their homes for dinner on several occasions. On the train, we always supported each other. (Conductors are automatically U.S. deputy marshals while on duty.) I had a special bond with Mr. Dale Braden of the Milwaukee Railroad. Although he was only 5'4" tall, he saved my goose during one particularly tense situation. I had confiscated several fifths of whiskey from two burly sailors and they had come after me with "blood in their eyes." They had backed me up against a bulkhead on the apron between two cars. I thought I could handle one of them, but two presented problems. Then Braden appeared.

"This is _my_ train and I'm a U.S. deputy Marshall," Braden shouted as he stepped between us. "Now get back in your seats by the count of ten, or I'm pulling this emergency cord and kicking your sailor-asses off the train, where there's nothing but jack rabbits and sage brush." They retreated like whipped puppies. Afterwards I laughed inwardly. Even with Braden's arm fully extended, there was a gap of two feet between his hand and the emergency cord!

For the most part my train rides went smoothly. Many of the servicemen wore the "yellow ruptured duck" on their uniforms, indicating they had been discharged and were on their way home. Most did not want to screw up, although now and then I encountered someone who wanted to make a final payment to me to even the score for some past real or imagined military injustice. Those who had been drinking were relatively easy to handle. Once I had to knock down a sailor who charged me. Another time I broke a nose. "Had trouble both ways this time," I wrote Father on February 23, 1946. "Knocked down a soldier who told me he would whip me if I got off the train. He had the right attitude after that." I wrote, "On March 12, I had a big fight with a machinist mate l/c; he was sober and tough and just back from overseas. I finally got a combination arm-lock and strangle-hold on him, which quieted him down."

If a troublemaker claimed he was a civilian, albeit still in uniform, I wired ahead for a civilian policeman to meet me at the next station. The silence was pervasive as we marched down the aisle to confront the malefactor. There was no escape, for we represented the two worlds of law enforcement. The police always agreed with my suggestion: "Put him in a cell for 24 hours until he cools off and then shove him on the next train." Although many police officers were as old as my Father, I appreciated the respect they gave me as a 19-year-old kid. Our uniforms cemented our bond--we were dedicated to uphold peace and order, the foundation of all cultural achievement.

While MPs carried Colt .45-caliber automatic pistols, Navy regulations allowed SPs to wear side-arms only when we were transporting prisoners. Sometimes I felt rather impotent with only an arm band, leggings, belt and a 16-inch billy club (the contemporary term is baton.) My billy was made of teak wood and had the weight of a lead pipe. I tried to overcome the paucity of my enforcement hardware by maintaining a proper military bearing and looking as serious and officious as I could.

Although I felt a bit defenseless in tight situations, I agreed with the restriction against carrying the Colt 45. The .45-caliber pistol is extremely lethal, and even a properly aimed round might ricochet around a train car and injure--or kill--innocent people. Besides, even a .45 was not a guarantee of safety. An MP friend was ambushed by half a dozen soldiers and thrown off the rear end of the Northern Pacific in North Dakota. The conductor said the train was going 90 miles an hour.

Fortunately, a seasoned SP had told me to carry a blackjack. I secured a good one that was made of leather, seven inches long, and properly bulbous on the end from its six ounces of lead shot. Normally I kept it out of sight on my back, behind the lacing of my pants. In tense situations I placed it under my sleeve where, with a flip of my wrist, it would be in my hand. It gave me tremendous psychic protection, even though I never had to use either it or my teakwood billy during my service as a Shore Patrolman. It would have cold-cocked even the toughest miscreant. I would have been court marshaled had anyone at Shore Patrol headquarters known I was carrying it.

Controlling liquor was the key to having a peaceful train. Liquor was the preferred anesthetic for many sailors during a cross-continental run. Inventive if not heroic attempts were made to bring it aboard. Minot, North Dakota, was always troublesome because the city tolerated bootleggers. As my trains pulled in, a half-dozen taxi cabs would be sitting on the station apron, their drivers selling hard liquor out of the trunks. The MP and I would hit the ground running and try to turn back an avalanche of servicemen headed for the taxis by shouting (falsely), "This area is off limits." Sometimes it felt like trying to divert Lemmings from their headlong rush to the sea.

Fighting on the train was directly proportional to the amount of booze on board. I confiscated each bottle I saw but promised the owners, "I'll lock this in my cabinet and you'll get it back at the end of your trip." Most of the time it worked.

I rode with some interesting MPs. One, Sergeant John McCarthy worked out of Fargo; after we had surveyed our train, we would sit in the conductor's alcove and regale each other with the "tough trains" we had had since the last time we rode together. John would recite to me some of the thousands of dirty stories-- "Benji, have you heard this one?"--he had memorized. I rode with him many times and never heard the same joke twice.

I was ashamed, however, to walk the aisle with Corporal Art Bussy. Bussy was only 5'6" but, in over-compensating for his short stature, he often acted like a Storm Trooper. Once he hit a defenseless and slightly tipsy private who had left his troop train and was trying to make out with a beautiful redhead. He was sweet-talking her when, without provocation or warning, Bussy hit him on the neck with his baton as hard as he could. I was embarrassed to be in his company but could not undercut his authority in the presence of civilians and other military. Later I reported the incident to my superiors and I told them I would not ride with him any more.

As winter turned to spring, my depression increased. Easter found me on the rails while my officers were home eating ham with their families. Still, for the most part I was all right when I was on duty; but being on liberty was tough. Each edition of *The Pipestone Star* reminded me that more of my friends were resuming their civilian lives. Bob had received an early discharge and was at Hamline University. Kenny Gibson, a crew mate from gunnery school days, was discharged early because his father could no longer farm. I felt sorry for myself. I didn't have the right story. No matter how I added up my points, I couldn't make them grow. Overseas duty would have compounded their number. By April I still had only 26-1/2 points. It meant I would have to wait until the end of July. Even my promotion to Aviation Radioman Second class, a new stripe, and an extra 18 dollars a month, only temporarily relieved my sense of hopelessness.

Some of my crew-mates had "re-upped" after trying civilian life for a few months. Civilian jobs were scarce, and those who re-enlisted within 90 days could retain their former rates. Calvin Peterson, an aviation ordnance man from Ohio, had been unable to find anything better than shoveling coal. As one of the masses of the unemployed, he had joined the "52/20 club"--52 weeks of $20-a-week welfare. "Benji, you don't know how hard it is out there," he protested. "There are no jobs worth having. I'm going to be a 'lifer.' At least you have a bed, three squares a day, clothes, medical care, and retirement." I considered him a lazy slob. Maybe those who choose to stay in the military during peacetime really *were* dogs. The Navy wasn't going to control my future; I had already filled out an application for Hamline University. Later, I realized Peterson's tale of hardship had not been exaggerated. The rapid shift from a wartime to peacetime economy created significant unemployment.

Meanwhile, my courtship with Jeanne was proceeding. She was a high-spirited girl with many interests. We played golf, bowled, rode horseback along Lake Michigan, went swimming and fishing, attended the theater and saw films by the score. Her favorite pastime was dancing, especially at the Aragon Ballroom at Lawrence Avenue near Broadway on Chicago's north side. The Aragon was reputed to be the most beautiful dance pavilion in the world. It was a romantic place and the famous big bands played there quite often. The make-believe stars, moon, and moving clouds above us were close replicas of the real thing. The ambiance was so close to perfection that most couples were in deep clinches as they danced. Despite the romantic atmosphere, however, and because I was a poor dancer and tickets were expensive, I was a reluctant participant.

Jeanne was a fine girl and I liked her a lot. Unfortunately, she was more serious than I was, and wanted more out of our relationship than I did. She was through with her schooling while I had not yet begun. Jeanne promised to wait for me no matter how many years my college and professional education might take. I stiff-armed her as gently as I knew how. I simply had too many future unknowns to make many promises. We had met at the wrong place and at the wrong time. I promised her that, after I was discharged, she could meet my family and together we would spend a week at Kee Nee Moo Sha. It was altogether too small a token of gratitude to her and her family for the love and hospitality they had shown me. She wanted much more and I felt bad.

By June my train trips had been shortened, some were solo, and there were fewer servicemen aboard. On June 12, 1946, I was transferred to the Navy Pier, which I described in a letter as "a real hole! It's a return to triple-decker bunks, cement floors, and rats as big as small dogs." A rat bit one of my friends and he had to go to the hospital. The pigeons and sparrows flew in and out as they pleased. I felt sorry for the guys on the top bunks whose blankets caught the bird droppings. The chow was terrible and I spent some nights at the YMCA and at the Walkers' house.

Added to my general distress was the apprehension raised by a June 10, 1946 letter from the Hamline Admissions office, which read as follows:

We have received your application for admission and your transcript of high school grades, and we are pleased to note that you ranked in the upper half of your class. However, your aptitude test scores fall somewhat below our requirement for admission. We would therefore suggest that you come to the campus whenever it is convenient to take another test. We have reason to believe that you will do satisfactorily on this test.
                    Sincerely yours,

            Alice M. Olson
            Secretary

Nine

Airman to Academia

The spring and summer of 1946 saw a pell-mell, hell-for-leather mob surging for the exit door from the services. As time passed, it began to seem as if every one of my high school classmates had gotten out. Then, finally, the magic day came. On July 24, I was placed in charge of 35 Navy personnel for a train-ride to the Great Lakes Naval Station. After three days of processing, we entrained for the Naval Air Station at the Wold-Chamberlain field in Minneapolis. I guarded the group's orders with my life. With the clock at 2359 hours, I didn't want to screw up now. I had written Hamline University that as soon as I was discharged, I would stop by and take the test that, hopefully, would qualify me for admission.

After running a gauntlet of tests and prodding, on July 28, my sister Martha's birthday, with my discharge papers in hand, I took a streetcar up St. Paul's Snelling avenue to Hamline University. The next day, totally out of my element, as a macho ex-Shore Patrolman, I walked timidly into Dr. Arthur Williamson's office to take a battery of tests.

I was directed to the library for what proved to be a three-hour ordeal. I could not have foreseen then that, exactly 20 years later, I would begin a 28 year career as a Hamline professor in an office 15 feet away.

The test was incredibly difficult. There was no way to circumvent my modest genetic inheritance nor to quickly overcome the damage inflicted on my education by the well-meaning but untrained homemakers who had been my substitute teachers in high school. What had happened to my mind during my sojourn in the Navy Air Corps? Bob came in, shook his head in empathy, worried with me, and left. I was lost.

I flagellated myself without mercy for the time I had wasted. Why had I not studied during the last two years? If only I had undertaken a reading program or registered for a correspondence course while I was in the Navy! Now it was too late. I shook my head as truisms-- "Time waits for no man" . . . "Seize the day" . . . "The march of history moves on"--popped into my head. Excuses, too, surfaced in my mind as easily as porpoises rise for air. "Damn the Navy and its fun and games," I quietly lamented. "It has ruined me." I wondered whether I should guess at the questions I could not answer. If my answer was wrong, would it be held against me? I did not know. In my anxiety I had not asked.

Ideas and excuses ricocheted around inside my head like the white marble in a Miles City pinball machine. I started planning an apology I would offer to Father when I returned home. Why had he not shunted his second-born into a vocation that corresponded with his modest I.Q. and capacities? I wondered, Were there any decent jobs in Pipestone? What could I do to avoid any further disgrace to the good name of Benjamin? Were there any junior colleges or trade schools that would have me? If I could not work with my brain, could I work with my hands? Where would I find surcease? Where could I find a haven in my time of trouble? Was there no place to hide?

I caught myself day-dreaming when I should have been concentrating. Dr. Williamson had looked like a kind man. His thin hair was parted in the middle. His professorial rimless glasses were precariously stuck half way down his nose, but his face had been expressive and warm. Did his utilitarian three-piece suit, with its Depression-era shine, disclose an empathy for the underdog? Could I tell him that I was "having a bad day" or that "my mind suddenly went blank?" Or had he heard these excuses many times before? Maybe I had too quickly judged the Navy. Should I return to Chicago and plead my case for re-admission as a lifer?

I rested my head on my hands. Without being aware of it, my doodling had covered my scratch paper. There were no recognizable images. The clock kept on ticking.

At a few minutes before noon, I put down my pencil and gathered up the papers. My Waterloo had taken place at Hamline. I was defeated not in a Privateer or on the Great Northern. Confronting a radio set, radar set, machine gun, or Navy thugs, I had proved my mettle but here I was humiliated. Oh, the shame of it all--to be so strong in body and so weak in mind! To be defeated by a stupid test. Father's motto came to mind: "It's not what happens to a man that counts. It's how he takes it." Such powerful words in the abstract! They did not touch my anguish. I walked slowly back to Dr. Williamson's office, with the shuffling steps of an old man with cerebral atrophy. He was out to lunch, but the secretary said, "Come back at 2:00 p.m.; we'll have your test corrected by then. Dr. Williamson will want to speak with you." There was little doubt as to what he would tell me.

In a daze I walked across Snelling Avenue to meet Bob for lunch. I chewed my food without tasting it. We spoke briefly about Kee Nee Moo Sha, the corn crop, and the weather. But mostly there was silence. Mercifully, he did not ask me how I did. Life was so unfair. The life of Joe College that I had hungered for during my years in the Navy was never to be. My vision of collegiate life was that of an academic promised land I would never reach. It was the dividing line between those who worked with their hands and those who used their gray matter. I lamented the fact that I had too little of the latter to escape using the former.

Bob's life, on the other hand, was on course as it had always been. His career was up, up, and away, like a jet-assisted Privateer rising from the runway. In contrast, mine had been dashed during those three hours just past, much like the explosion of a TBY torpedo bomber falling into the sea.

At 2:00 p.m. I returned to Dr. Williamson's office in Old Main. I had fortified myself for the news of my rejection. Dr. Williamson saw me coming down the hall. I was surprised that he got up from behind his desk with my papers in his hand. A fleeting thought crossed my mind that he wanted to give me the bad news in the hallway and out of the hearing of the secretary. As a kind man he would want to minimize my embarrassment and pain.

But Dr. Williamson stepped in front of his desk and smiled as I entered the office. An epiphany was about to begin! He extended his hand in greeting. "Walter, let me offer you my congratulations," he said warmly, "you will do well. You will be an excellent student. We are proud to have you as a member of the Hamline family."

War and Reflection:
A Half Century Later

As I study the faces of students in my college classes, I am sometimes greatly tempted to warn them that they have not the slightest idea of what they are capable. This rational dialogue we are carrying on together is likely to seem to some of the sheltered ones the dependable face of reality. Yet I need only close my eyes to imagine those faces contorted with hatred, those hands, feminine or masculine, clenched or clawlike, those bodies tensed and ready to spring, in order to realize that all of us conceal, half-knowing, powers that are at the furthest removed from the present setting.
    J. Glenn Gray, <u>On Understanding Violence Philosophically</u>

To the end of history, the peace of the world, as Augustine observed, must be gained by strife. It will therefore not be a perfect peace. But it can be more perfect than it is. If the mind and the spirit of man does not attempt the impossible, if it does not seek to conquer or to eliminate nature, but tries only to make the forces of nature the servants of the human spirit and the instruments of the moral ideal, a progressively higher justice and more stable peace can be achieved.
    Reinhold Niebuhr, <u>Moral Man and Immoral Society</u>

Dr. Rieux knew that the tale he had to tell could not be one of a final victory. It could only be the record of what had had to be done, and what assuredly would have to be done again in the never ending fight against terror and its relentless onslaughts . . . by all who, while unable to be saints but refusing to bow down to pestilences, strive their utmost to be healers. (Rieux knew) that there are more things to admire in man than to despise.
    Albert Camus, <u>The Plague</u>

Introduction

A glacial shift has occurred regarding the place and role of the military since I served 50 years ago. Nostalgia aside, I am one of millions of veterans who, having been lucky enough to escape being killed or severely injured, view their military experience as largely positive. Despite all the frustration and dislocation, I, like millions of my peers, left the service with a strength and maturity that I did not have when I entered. I am quite sure that, had I entered college at the age of 17, without the experience and maturity gained in the Navy, I would have flunked out. Chronologically, my age had advanced only two years; emotionally, I was closer to a decade older.

I sometimes watch a late night movie from that era. Giants walked the Hollywood turf during the 1940s-- Alan Ladd, Gregory Peck, Cary Grant, Clark Gable, John Wayne, Alice Faye, Rita Hayworth, Betty Grable. Directors appealed to the saintly rather than the bestial elements of our being. The motives of discipline, sacrifice, honor, vision, promise-keeping and duty were fortissimo. The lyrics of our popular songs and ballads were wistful, romantic, hopeful, and affirmative. One simply cannot find rape, obscenity, pornography, incivility, crudity, or nudity in the films of my youth and of that era. Even the depictions of violence against the Japanese and Germans tended to be antiseptic, ritualized, and distanced.

Fifty years later, that stable world of my upbringing is almost gone. The cultural barbarians seem to have penetrated the gates of our civitas. Does age work a double effect upon our memory--enlarging the positive while diminishing the negative experiences of our youth? Is my angst, after living nearly the Biblical three score and ten years, just a figment of my twilight ruminations? Perhaps, but the hard empirical data attesting to our increasing personal and social pathologies cannot be avoided.

I fear for my grandchildren in ways my parents never had to fear for their children.

During World War II and through the 1950s, our nation was unified by communal goals and a shared direction. While we knew there were imperfections such as racism and poverty that sullied the American Experiment, such problems neither traumatized nor defined us. Hopeful realism rather than nihilism, optimism rather than cynicism, characterized the ethos of that era.

I wish that I could endow the youth of this generation with my Navy experience. To that end the second half of this volume seeks to interpret some of the powerful social forces of the 1960s, campus traumas, the ethics of coercion, pacifism, and the draft. I'll also seek to examine the role of the academy, the ethics of Hiroshima, the Japanese military, and other lessons from history. Those of us whose hair has grayed have had a different and longer journey than those still in their teens and twenties. In its most simple rendering, the term "veteran," indicates a unique window of experience, unknown to those who never went through that rite of passage. While age does not automatically convey wisdom, it is also true that the freshness and innocence of youth are seldom balanced by the prudence and discernment, the circumspection and discretion, that often come with increasing years. Every 60-year-old was once 20. A twenty-year-old, however, has *not* been 60.

While youth often dismisses or makes fun of the wrecks of old age, I believe it is important to hear the stories and lessons of past generations. History reveals a cyclicism where, under different costumes and disguises, the demons of despotism appear and reappear. In truth, the early 20th century was a time when monsters marched across the nations, and the earth trembled. Before the end of the most bloody century in history, and before funeral homilies have been delivered for the remaining veterans of World War II, we need to learn as much as we can from them.

Two-and-a-half decades after my military experience concluded, the traditional mythology of war sustained by poet, sage, and patriot was nearly gone. Until recently, the West derived its martial ethic from Homer's *Iliad*. Combat was celebrated in close quarters, between comparably armed male warriors, on neutral ground, far from women and children. Individual virtues such as bravery and strength, not weapons, won the day. Hence the Homeric hero's disdain for the bow: "My way is not to fight my battles standing far way from my enemies."

Until 1914, according to George Will, the military was the last redoubt of romantics in the industrial age. Then the machine gun enabled "three men and a gun to stop a battalion of heroes." Military romantics--who are not an endangered species, but a vanished one, buried in Flanders Fields--regretted the machine gun and likewise would have regretted the "smart" bomb and Tomahawk missile because "you can't pin a medal on a piece of metal." But neither need you bury a piece of metal in Arlington Cemetery.

Thus, nobility and honor have become unfashionable in our time. "Alas," wrote Carlyle, "the hero of old has had to cramp himself into strange places: the world knows not well at any time what to do with him, so foreign is his aspect to the world." Churchill once observed that "war, which was always cruel and glorious, has become cruel and sordid."

Video cameras and satellite astro hook-ups have made it possible to transmit the gruesome reality of war straight to the living rooms of the American family--live, as it's happening. Medieval canvasses and poetry portrayed war in epic proportions, its combatants as heroes of classic stature. No more. Until this tragic and bloody century, the profession of arms had always been crowned with honor and virtue. But now both war and the warrior have been demystified and profaned by technology. Unlike former eras, in this one it is difficult if not impossible to portray war as a Homeric encounter. War has become far too gory an undertaking to consider participation "a red badge of courage" rite of passage in the earning of one's manhood.

And too accessible. The reality of combat--mud, tears, destruction, bodies, napalm, refugees, suffering, crying, naked children, burning thatched huts--is now instantaneously available in living color. Only the smell is missing.

The decade of the 1960s was a tragic one because it saw the erosion of the traditionally strong, positive emotional bonds that Americans historically have had with their country. The cultural elites--from Hollywood film makers to editorial writers, from academic intellectuals to commercial artists and novelists--saw the Vietnam war as proof positive that the American Experiment was vitiated to its core. Vietnam turned legions of college youth into "Amerika"-hating radicals. To them the police were "pigs," an occupying force employed by venal capitalist tyrants to pacify the unruly urban colonies. In England a Rhodes Scholar and future American president was an artful dodger of the draft. In a 1969 letter to the head of the ROTC program at the University of Arkansas, Bill Clinton said he and his

Introduction 93

friends "loathed" the military. Sadly enough, that sentiment was very popular at the time. Later in the White House, one of Clinton's administrative aides is said to have remarked, upon meeting an officer from the Pentagon, "I don't speak to people in uniforms."

Clearly, a portentous change had occurred in the years separating my world and Mr. Clinton's.

Ten

Vignettes Of Campus Culture In The Sixties

Youth: Bearers of a Messianic Future?

One of the most important books attesting to a significant change in student attitude and behavior during the Vietnam era was Charles Reich's *The Greening of America* (1970). Reich, a professor of law at Yale University, looked beyond student strikes, campus chaos, and disastrous confrontations like the one at Kent State to a coming new and glorious era. Beneath the dirty, undisciplined, and drug-addicted students he saw flower-children, the midwives of a messianic age. Hundreds of thousands of copies of the book were sold and Reich became the intellectual guru of the counter-cultural college crowd.

History offers some perspective on those who would baptize adolescents and make them the bearers of utopian dreams made incarnate. The rapacity of the Industrial Revolution induced many philosophers and men of letters wistfully to postulate an original "state of nature," in which natives were unspoiled, communal, and pure in body, soul, and human relations. Anthropologists sought to find such uncorrupted "children of nature" in islands and lands where capitalism had as yet not penetrated. Youth, especially, represented an immaculate Rosseau-like innocence: "How is it that man is born free, but is everywhere in chains?" Culture, especially that of the West, does not liberate but corrupts us, according to this view.

Totalitarians, especially Marxists and Fascists, have always enlisted young people to be the harbingers of communal utopias. An adolescent is a *tabula rasa*, a "blank state" in need of band wagons to climb on and demons to vilify. Youths need heroes to adulate and causes to fight for. Thus, their loyalties are often fickle and as psychologically malleable as silly-putty. Their minds are not constrained by tradition, doctrine, prejudice, zero-sum trade-offs, and a "bear and bull" cyclicism, not only of the market but of life itself. Seeking a certitude that no finite loyalty can provide, they are uncomfortable with a presentation that states, "On the one hand *this*, on the other hand *that*." Thus, soft totalitarians isolate their elders to prevent their cynicism--"*that's been tried* before and it *doesn't work*"--from corrupting adolescent indoctrination. Hard totalitarians simply shoot recalcitrant seniors or put them in Gulags.

But the attractiveness of Reich's revelation is that totalitarians, whether soft or hard, are not needed to transform our society. Our flower children are the vanguard of a new marvelous era. A New World will be ushered in by grace, not violence. The pupils can teach their mentors! The Biblical dictum--"And a child shall lead them"-- was deemed to have come true in America in the 60s.

Reich divided the American Experience into three types of consciousness:

Consciousness I began with the landing of the Puritans and continued until the Great Depression. "Con I" is the traditional outlook of the American farmer, small businessman, and worker trying to get ahead. Positively, its virtues are plainness, character, honesty, thrift, and hard work. The underside of Con I is self-interest, competitiveness, suspicion of others, guilt, and selfishness. It is suspicious of human nature. Grant Wood's classic painting, "American Gothic," encapsulates the soul of Con I folk. The Iowa couple, pitchfork in hand, stand before their barn. They radiate the solitariness and the suspicion of their pinched lives. A wag might comment, "they look like they were weaned on a pickle." Consciousness I is psychologically constipated. Constitutionally introverted emotions do not flow freely. Like many of the ideological offspring of Benjamin Franklin, they seem to be "fat of purse but thin of soul."

Reich seems to be describing my kin folk on both sides. Indeed, until he enlightened me about their benighted souls, I had thought I came from fairly sound stock!

It was a hell-of-a-run while it lasted, but Con I collapsed with the Great Depression. Con I's faith in technology, market forces, and laissez-faire led to monstrous consequences: "robber barons, business piracy, ruinous competition, unreliable products and false advertising, grotesque inequality, and the chaos of excessive individualism and lack of coordination and planning, leading to a gangster world." After 200 years of brilliant, unmatched progress, Con I has exhausted our collective soul and soil. Our forests are denuded; rivers and lakes polluted; cities sterile; land ripped by highways, high tension wires, and suburban swaths. It is time for a psychic revolution. But Con I folk can't change and many are still with us today. They think America still consists of farms and stereotypical "Our Towns" of the heartland. They don't know it yet, but as Mark Twain put it, "The Great Barbecue" is over.

Consciousness II came with the savior of the 1930s--Franklin Delano Roosevelt. The New Deal rose like a phoenix from the ashes of the Great Depression. A liberal legacy and genealogy--Harry Truman, Adlai Stevenson, John and Bobby Kennedy, Lyndon Johnson, Hubert Humphrey--initiated far-reaching reforms. A social contract and safety net that protected minorities, women, farmers, and labor and controlled the uses of capital came into existence.

Alas, as the 60s proved, in its act of taming the capitalist Corporate State of Con I, Con II created an even greater monster, the public Corporate State. Hierarchical elitism shifted from the corporation to the State. Lawyers, "experts," "consultants," "policy scientists," "social engineers" settled within the Washington beltway and pulled up the drawbridge. Con II people are "institutional" robots whose motto is "Ask what you can do for your country (and corporation)." Reform was on the surface. Mere political change, alterations of law, in structure or in government power, did not accomplish real reform.

There are no intractable dilemmas for Con II, no intractable problems at all if science, technology, organization, planning, and logic are applied by the mentally gifted. A democratic aristocracy of merit-based rational standards will lead us into the promised land of abundance for all, according to this view. The perennial afflictions of Homo Sapiens--cancer, poverty, homelessness, racism, war, ignorance, crime and more-- will fall one-by-one, like dominoes. But be careful--this will only happen if the latest state-of-the-art technology is used and Ivy League graduates are employed.

The final symbol of Con II bankruptcy, of course, was the inability of Secretary of Defense Robert MacNamara and all of his "Whiz Kids" to "manage" the Vietnam war. Rice-eating peasants wearing black pajamas and shod with flip-flops were victorious over the most powerful Corporate State and military machine the world had ever known.

At this critical juncture, Reich looked out his window and his students graced him with a revelation! He observed in them a *psychic and moral mutation.* This dramatic change--**Consciousness III**--would spare

America a bloody revolution. With the rare exception of the Weatherman faction of the Students for a Democratic Society, students were not attempting to destroy the Corporate State. Rather, they were simply detouring around Con I's selfishness and Con II's statism. *They are simply walking away!* Joe College and Suzy Coed are simply repeating an ancient pattern that, in the western world, is traceable to the early Christian Church.

In the fifth century, many youngsters of the elite Roman classes, fed up with the nihilism of *la dolce vita*, exited the social, economic, and political affairs of the Empire. To their elder's exhortations--"be practical," "the Empire needs you," "prepare for a good job"--like our hippies, they answered, "take a hike." The Establishment was rotten. Why should they attempt to revivify an unburied corpse? Sir Edward Gibbon, author of the classic, *The Decline and Fall of the Roman Empire*, accused the Church of sapping the vital juices of the Empire by encouraging the "brightest and best" to eschew political service for monastic virtue. They knew the Empire was *in extremis.*

Thus, our flower children are re-enacting a classic pattern of social revolution--institutions are changed as much by leaving as by confrontation. Youthful artists, poets, and balladeers have sensitive antennae. Their poems and songs reveal exotic geographic and psychic journeys. They hear a different drummer and march to a different beat. Their jeans, beards, beads, tie-dyed shirts, sandals, functional clothing, natural colors, shoulder-length hair and more reveal an instinctual altruism, earthiness and love of nature.

Tragically, Con I and II people are deaf and blind to the messages from the ether picked up by the intuitive eyes and ears of Con III students. But they will change. A "peaceable kingdom" is coming much like that represented in "old American paintings that show all manner of beasts lying down together in harmony and love." Where Brook Farm, the Oneida Community and the Shakers failed, Con III communities will sprout up like "flowers through the asphalt," Reich asserts. Then <u>Walden II</u> will be more than a behaviorist's dream.

Consciousness III advocates know that no politics, doctrine, ideology, structure, or system of government can give happiness and meaning. Flower children follow a simple mantra--"tune in, turn on, drop out." The commune is their Bethlehem, Woodstock their Easter, the common marijuana joint their sacramental host, tie-died clothes their vestments. The power of the Corporate State will be destroyed by "living differently." But I cannot help but wonder whether Reich wrote the following with a straight face:

> The plan, the program, the grand strategy, is this: resist the State, when you must; avoid it, when you can; but listen to music, dance, seek out nature, laugh, be happy, be beautiful, help others whenever you can, work for them as best you can, take them in, the old and the bitter as well as the young, live fully in each moment, love and cherish each other, love and cherish yourselves, stay together.

Since the Corporate State rests on nothing but "consciousness," that is, a set of mental images, its present foundations are crumbling badly. When consciousness changes, soldiers will refuse to fight, police will rebel, bureaucrats will stop working, and jailers will unlock the cells. Even businessmen, when liberated, will "roll in the grass and lie in the sun." "Nothing can stop the power of consciousness."

In critique, I must say that, however brilliant Charles Reich may have been as a professor of torts, as a social philosopher, he deserves an "F." The angle of vision determines what one sees. From my prism in the 60s, I saw a darkening, not a greening, of America. From his law school window, he may have desperately wanted to see something positive in his frolicking, dissolute, frisbee-tossing students. Were they living the spontaneous and carefree life he never had as a youth? As a tenured member of the Yale law faculty (could any position be a more integral part of the Corporate State than that?) did he hunger for a "secular conversion" and a community bond that the Yale quadrangle could not provide?

I have no desire, however, to psychoanalyze Reich or to question his motives. It is enough to evaluate his vision--ideas I find fanciful at best and dangerous at worst. His ridicule of middle America led campus radicals to reject the character-forming events--the Depression, war, job-holding, the daily struggles of immigrant families--that shaped the values of their elders. His attack on the formation of *character* (sobriety, probity, work as a calling), according to Stephen Haseler in *The Varieties of Anti-Americanism*, broke the bow of moral action among the poor who up until then had emulated the middle class. Work became a curse. Gone was the puritan imperative that held it was valued not only for itself but also as the engine for economic growth. From the ramparts of Yale and with little empirical data, Reich pontificates:

> Work and living have become more and more pointless and empty. For most Americans work is mindless, exhausting, boring, servile, and hateful. Our life activities have become plastic, vicarious, and false to our genuine needs, activities fabricated by others and forced upon us.

Perhaps Reich tells us more about himself than about America during the 1960s.

Clearly Reich hates modernity and can be charged with archaism. He represents the periodic return to the romantic motif of the "noble savage" that runs through the writings of Irving, Cooper, Schoolcraft, and Longfellow and that coexisted in complex if antidotal relation to the Indian-hating metaphysics of Jackson, Harrison, and Crockett. Reich sees his students, like the uncorrupted children of nature, as living within themselves, not artificially and outside themselves. Our Yale professor was one of the first in the academy to succumb to radical chic.

Reich seems to long for a time without technology, industrialism, and the modern state. With the collapse of the Corporate State, he argues, anarchistic sects or "therapeutic communities" will spring up and perform the functions now provided by the family, church, volunteer societies, and the neighborhood. His criticism of technology and industry has Luddite tendencies; it would be interesting to know whether he bought a personal computer when they came on the market in the 80s.

The Greening of America holds that communities can be created via fervent moralisms about "living free in love." His apostles on other campuses did not critique hippie blather--"yea drugs and revolution, boo war and corporate profits" and "bust the pigs." Reich should have studied the Catholic monastic movement. It has a record of success that spans 15 centuries. The building blocks of successful communes are discipline, faith, written constitutions, common worship, virtue, character, asceticism, sacrifice, and hard work. Hippie communes were short-lived because their members had a paucity of personal capital. They were long on political talk and drugs, short on milking cows and shoveling manure. Even communes have to worry about that Con II "mark of Cain," the bottom line. But Reich's cardinal error was his assumption that a group (in his case, students) is mysteriously exempt from what theologians and psychologists call respectively, original sin and the ego-centric predicament. Reich is a member of a long line of romantics and idealists who have given a messianic mantle to a race, religion, denomination, gender, or ethnic collective. Can any gathering, however intelligent, spiritual, or chaste, exempt itself from the historical conditioning factors of its era? No. To assume that a particular community is morally superior to all others is not only patently false but dangerous. Any group, whether fascists, feminists, Marxists, Christians, or "greening" students, that believes it is the bearer of a this-world millennium, has the potential to become totalitarian. Reich and his apostles were of little help in giving students perspective. Many coveted the accolades of students and seldom let a faculty meeting go by without pontificating, *"I'm for student's rights!"* Some made a grim attempt to hang on to their youth by adopting not only the wardrobe of the street people but also their long hair, profanity, ideology, and hatred of the administration. They seldom let a student-generated petition cross their desks without signing it. Seemingly unaware of their impotence, they thought their signature had the weight of John Hancock's.

Today the ideological offspring of *Greening* tell us that women, Native Americans, blacks, homosexuals, or some other "marginalized group" has a corner on enlightenment and virtue. Internationally, youth-as-messiah movements have been identified with everything from Castro's guerrillas and the Sandinistas, to Pol Pot's butchers and the vicious Morning Star movement in Peru. In every generation there are Charles Reichs who, in lamenting injustice, cast the mantle of savior on the shoulders of the young. Mussolini's fascist youth brigades sang with gusto as they marched through Rome:
Spring Time, Spring Time,

> All Hail to our Glorious Spring Time,
> We, the Youth Are With You, Il Duce,
> We are the Bearer and Vision of the Future.

Of all segments of the Third Reich, William Shirer observed that it was the Nazi university youth who sang the "Horst Wessle Song" with the greatest gusto.

Unlike Reich, I refused to view collegiate youth of the 60s through rose-colored glasses. Like Jack McCall in Pat Conroy's <u>Beach Music</u>, I observed that "the facile and the cheap became celebrated and the speech of idiots took on a beknighted, kingly quality." I saw the wreckage that Reich's clap-trap made of many student lives. Underneath their bravado many students were miserable, spoiled, demanding, intolerant, ill-disciplined, and useless to either themselves or their country. They saw and magnified, as did too many of their mentors, all the warts on *Amerika*. They were blind to the freedoms, rights, and affluence of America and Western culture.

(The "greening" virus, however, infected fewer majors in the natural sciences than those in the humanities and social sciences. The former tended to have more conservative professors and to be more earnest and sure of their career track.)

In the late 60s I noticed that Kent, one my favorite students, had poor footwear. He used duct tape and twine to tie the soles of his shoes to the uppers. "Take this twenty-dollar bill," I pleaded, "get yourself a serviceable pair of shoes at Goodwill." He sheepishly declined. Later I discovered his father owned a shoe factory in Milwaukee.

Many young people of the 60s gave up vocational goals, became promiscuous, turned into acid-heads, gave up medical or business college in favor of making sandals and belts, held deans and presidents captive, joined a cult and became brain-washed, disowned their parents, and much more. Cynicism grew apace. "The

Establishment" was the radicals' demon, but most knew precious little of the off-campus world. For many the slogan--"Never trust anyone *over thirty*"--culminated in self-hatred. It left them cocooned in adolescent fantasy without the leaven of perspective and experience that the elders of every generation provide for the next generation. Hundreds of thousands made tragic and life-stultifying choices.

Occasionally, I run into former students who were disciples of Reich. I inwardly weep for most of them, of what they might have been. When a wrong turn is made at a crucial time in life, it is hard to get back on track and fulfill one's potential. Some were able to overcome their "greening" sojourn, pick up the pieces, and achieve some belated success. A few even realized that a single middle-class business person can do more for society than hundreds of "greening" advocates pasting *VISUALIZE WORLD PEACE* bumper stickers on their cars. They might even agree with P. J. O'Rourke's comment in *Give War A Chance* that the Marine Corps does more to promote peace than all the Ben & Jerry's ice cream ever made.

O'Rourke, the satirist, looked back with amazement at his credulity as a flower child:

> You name it and I believed it. I BELIEVED love was all you need . . . drugs could make everyone a better person . . . I could hitchhike to California with thirty-five cents and people would be glad to feed me . . . Mao was cute . . . private property was wrong ... my girlfriend was a witch . . . my parents were Nazi space monsters . . . the university was putting saltpeter in the cafeteria food . . . stones had souls . . . the Viet Cong were the good guys in Vietnam . . . Lyndon Johnson was plotting to murder all the Negroes . . . Yoko Ono was an artist . . . Bob Dylan was a musician

> . . . I would live forever or until twenty-one, whichever came first . . . the world was about to end . . . the Age of Aquarius was about to happen . . . the *I Ching* said to cut classes and take over the dean's office . . . wearing my hair long would end poverty and injustice. *I believed there was a great throbbing web of psychic mucus and we were all part of it somehow. With the exception of anything my mom and dad said, I believed everything.*

When the traditional anchors of faith and ideals slip, a person is prone to believe too much rather than too little. An easy credulity is far more dangerous than a reverent agnosticism. A final word regarding Charles Reich: A wise professor once told me to never trust an author who reduces cultural complexity to three movements.

A March I Regret Taking

On a Saturday morning in April, 1969, while I was a professor of humanities at Hamline University in St. Paul, I joined a faculty-student group that marched on the Minnesota capital protesting the war in Vietnam. I was a reluctant marcher and had joined my colleagues and students out of a sense of guilt. To join a campus *cause celebre* was an easy avenue to student favor. Campus reputations were achieved by seeing how vociferously you could protest against "The Establishment." Out-of-the-closet conservative professors were scarce and were objects of scorn; the majority were in self-protective hibernation.

Our march had less order than Cox's army. We walked and skylarked through blue-collar neighborhoods east of the campus on our way to the capital. The working class homes were modest two-bedroom, 1100-

square-feet affairs, which would have sold then for about $30,000. The lawns, soft from April showers, were well-tended, and carefully groomed flowerbeds were just beginning to break through. As students trampled over their lawns and flowers, men in undershirts or blue working shirts came out and remonstrated with us. It was obvious that many were veterans of World War II and the Korean war. We were transgressing the turf of the urban ethnics or PIIGS--<u>P</u>olish, <u>I</u>rish, <u>I</u>talian, <u>G</u>reek, <u>S</u>lav--whose sons were bearing the consequences of our tragic and faltering foreign policy. Many of their homes flew the flag. In contrast many of our students had sewn Old Glory on the seat of their torn and faded jeans. One student carried the flag upside down, the military signal for distress. Others simply flittered along, hiding their affluence behind dirty and frayed clothes. While some male students had scraggly beards and hair that trailed down toward their waists, most of the homeowners were clean shaven; a few had even adopted their "high and tight" military crew-cuts in civilian life.

A verbal exchange began; "Stay on the <u>sidewalk</u>" was answered with "<u>Screw</u> yourself!" The altercation quickly escalated to shouting, name-calling, and hurling obscenities which, among the students, were employed by both genders. Raised middle fingers jabbed the air. Epithets directed toward the onlookers--"Archie Bunker," "Goon," "Moron," "Dummkopf," "Hard-hat," "Redneck," ---produced angry retorts from the home-owners--"Communist," "Traitor," "Sissy," "Yellow-livered," "Love It Or Leave It," "Radical!"

Shame overcame me. I became nauseated and feared I might lose my breakfast. I was in the wrong crowd! Yet, I did not have the courage to leave and join the working-class neighborhood residents on their porches. My desire to be accepted by my students and peers sullied my conscience. The coercive need to belong, to be loved and accepted as a member of a group, had diminished my power to stand alone. In my intellectual arrogance, I had joined a campus mob. Indeed, we were a self-righteous rabble. Why had I forgotten that crowds and mobs destroy rather than create?

How ironic that a movement intended to suture and heal our national wound was exacerbating the injury and making it more ugly. Although they were served less well by our nation than were my affluent students, the working people of our country were more honorable, authentic human beings.

Many of my students come from the suburban areas. Most had gone to fine public schools. At Hamline they were receiving an outstanding liberal arts education. Many would enter the professions. In contrast, an examination of the resumes of the workers would find their backgrounds to be quite modest--high school, trade school, apprenticeship, journeyman and union member. They appeared to be carpenters, plumbers, firemen, electricians, municipal workers, and the like. They may have made good money while they worked, but they often faced two or three months of enforced "vacations" when they were without paychecks. Their values were centered on the family, church, neighborhood, and America, a constellation of loyalties that many of my students believed were either unimportant, corrupt, or beneath them.

However strong student compassion might have been for Blacks, Hispanics, women, and homosexuals, they despised the blue-collar workers of America. They assumed those who carried a lunch bucket to work were bigoted, hard-hat Archie Bunkers. By affluence and IQ, deviousness, status, or just luck, the students avoided becoming citizen soldiers, leaving that job, and all its attendant risks, to the children of the less privileged classes. They salved their consciences by demonizing and hating those who worked in the mines, factories, and fields, who in fact, did America's scut work.

Special privileges make all persons dishonest. Many students viewed a military uniform as the mark of Cain. Many of our faculty seemed to agree, and military recruiters told me they experienced the "heart of the stranger" while on our campus. (Years later, because of the armed services' exclusion of out-of-the-closet homosexuals, recruiters could not set up their tables in the student center). Such childish mischief did not harm the armed services, which simply intensified their recruiting activities on community and state college campuses.

During my April "march for peace," two American worlds collided near my campus. What happened in our nearby ethnic neighborhood was but a microcosm of what transpired across our land. American labor, including the AF of L and the CIO, perceived the academy of which I was a part as unpatriotic, "dovish," self-righteous, contemptuous of their vocation, and unappreciative of their sacrifice both at home and abroad. Their antennae could detect a "I am more moral-than-thou" attitude however it might be camouflaged. Thus, in a classic case of the law of unintended consequences, "peace marches" tended to increase labors' militancy and hawkish stance regarding our Vietnam tragedy. Labor supported Presidents Johnson and Nixon right up until the end. Because academia did not care enough to understand and appreciate the American worker, it manifested little interest in coopting labor to support its agenda. For its part, labor returned the compliment by despising university protestors.

The result was less harmony, increased class conflict, and more hatred. I was ashamed of myself and regretted I had been party to such a charade. I promised myself to be more careful of the crowds I would join in the future.

A Relevant But Explosive Course

Several times during the Vietnam years I offered a course entitled "Revolution, Violence, and Conscience." I wanted to give ethical, philosophical, and historical perspective to the trauma of that era. We analyzed the psychological characteristics of major revolutions, the morality of coercion and war, rival theories concerning the nature of man, and historical issues regarding Vietnam. Once I invited a panel of recent Vietnam veterans to reflect on their experience to give a dose of realism to the course.

One of the panelists was Tom Anderson, 43, who represented a "crusade mentality" regarding war. An Army "lifer" of twenty years, he was studying for a second career--that of an Episcopal priest. He wanted to show colored photos he had taken of dozens of dead Viet Cong following the Tet offensive. I thought that inappropriate to the course. Tom had been untouched by the brutality he saw and photographed. Emotionally flat, he manifested little ambiguity about the war or his participation in it. (I wondered about his parents and teachers and what had happened in the shaping of his super-ego.) For Tom, Vietnam had been a holy war and he had become a warrior-automaton, totally untouched by the brutality, ambiguity, guilt, and tragedy of killing.

Another panelist, Steve Peterson, 23, had been an Army ranger. One day while on patrol, he was walking 15 feet behind his best friend, when suddenly a mine exploded and blew off his friend's leg, killing him. A "papa san" was planting rice 200 feet away at the time. "He must have known that mine was there," Steve loudly insisted; "Viet Cong swim through villages like fish in the ocean. They kill the teachers and elite of the community. That papa san knew about that mine and didn't tell us. He was responsible for the death of my friend. I wasted (shot) him." Then he broke down and could not continue. It was obvious that many of those who had survived physically had nevertheless become psychic victims.

Panelist Wayne Camp, 23, a former Marine, had joined the Corps because "The Marines are a Cadillac outfit. I would have a better chance of survival if I had the best training there is." After confronting the chaos of combat, Wayne, like most warriors, extended himself to orphans and refugees. Many medical professionals believe that such altruism represents a soldier's unconscious attempt to preserve his psychic equilibrium. Thus, whenever he was off duty, Wayne would go to an orphanage to give children candy and rations, and to play games with them. He became especially attached to a seven year-old girl named Kari whose parents, village teachers, had been killed by the Viet Cong. He thought about adopting her after the war, when he would be married.

On his last visit to the orphanage, the headmaster told him that Kari had been killed. She had fallen into a punji pit--a deep hole at the bottom of which were sharp bamboo spikes smeared with human excrement. A technique invented to trap and kill animals was being used by the Viet Cong to dispatch human prey.

"The next day," Wayne told the class in an even voice, "I personally killed five Viet Cong. I wanted revenge for her death."

A student with pacifist tendencies immediately jumped to his feet, pointed his finger at Wayne, and screamed, "You are truly a barbarian, a murdering son-of-a-bitch! How could you do such a thing?"

"Had you been there," Wayne answered quietly, "I have no doubt that you would have done the same thing."

John Pennel, 29, a former army captain who had been discharged because of his wounds, stated, "I made a difficult judgment call that proved to be wrong." Tears began to form in his eyes as he continued. "Some of my men died as a result of an ambush that I should have foreseen. I will carry the guilt of that decision to my grave."

The problem facing every commander, from Robert E. Lee in the Civil War through Dwight Eisenhower in World War II to Norman Schwarzkopf in Desert Storm in 1991, is how to motivate decent young men raised on moral precepts about the preciousness of human life and the immorality of killing to become efficient killing machines. Many clergy, mothers, and others inwardly cringe at the very thought. But good commanders are superb at training and motivating their warriors to survive by killing others. It is a cardinal moral issue. Sensitive commanders, like Atlas, bear an exceedingly heavy burden on their shoulders.

Eleven

Vignettes Of Campus Culture In The Sixties: II

Two Generations Collide Under the Flag Pole:

"I saw those students messing with the flag, and I covered the 200 feet from my classroom to the flag pole in nothing flat," reflected my colleague, Dick Mulkern, the Hamline University football coach. "The flag was on the ground and it looked as if they were either going to burn it or pee on it." College kids were getting their kicks by using the American flag to start fires along the boulevard.

Dick continued: "My neck veins were pumping and must have been the size of a garden hose. I recognized several people who were not Hamline students and I ordered them off the campus." Fortunately, both the students and non-students left. It was touch and go. "I was close to being out of control," Mulkern reflected. "Had I lost it, there would have been blood on the grass."

Later, in an act of cowardice, the dean of students removed the flag to prevent "an incident."

It was the year during which several students were killed during a war protest at Kent State University in Ohio. Pontificating from an academic island of self-righteous purity, our faculty had drafted a telegram urging President Nixon to unilaterally get out of Vietnam. Although there were a number who abstained, Mulkern and physics professor Kent Bracewell, were the only faculty who voted against sending the message.

Was Mulkern's dash to the flag pole an irrational confrontation between a jock coach and some bored students who wanted media attention? No, the issue is far more problematical than that. It illustrates the difficulty one generation has in transferring its commitments and values to its successor. Veterans of World War II, such as Mulkern and I, were a dying breed during Vietnam. No one knew or seemed to care about the origin of his loyalty to and defense of the flag.

Mulkern was a kid pilot of 20 in India and Burma during World War II. "We carried everything from dead bodies to Kotex in our C47 transports, the workhorses of the war." During missions into China, his air wing lost about 600 planes of all types--C47s, C46s, B25s, P47s, and P37s.

"January 5, 1945 was awful," Dick remembered. "We lost 45 planes that day. All day long the radio screamed, 'May Day, May Day!' Wind shears of 150 MPH slammed airplanes into mountain sides. Engines caught fire, electrical systems went out, and hydraulic systems malfunctioned. Violent down-drafts caused some planes to lose 5,000 feet within a minute. Usually bailing out of a plane that was in trouble was about as risky as trying to ride out the problem. More often than not a pilot who parachuted was killed in a rugged mountain landing or, if he survived that, was unable to live in the rugged and inhospitable terrain. Monsoons dumped over 400 inches of rain from March to October. Cobras and scorpions were always a threat and pilots fought depression, jungle rot, and dysentery. Even though I never had to 'hit the silk,' I went from 175 to 139 pounds in six months," Mulkern mused.

He usually flew solo. But once when a flight surgeon was riding shotgun, the plane was struck by lightning and barely missed a mountain. "He took a jeep back," Mulkern laughed. Then, more soberly, he noted, "In six months, 60 percent of my squadron was dead."

In Mulkern's view, people who desecrate the flag are not engaging in free speech. They are trashing the world and the symbol for which he and his fellow pilots sacrificed, suffered, and died. Radicalized students, on the other hand, deemed the flag but a sign, that is, a demonic emblem that revealed an "Amerika" that is rotten to the core. As such it became the focus of their animus.

A symbol is different in kind from a sign. A stop sign, an exit sign, or a honking car horn are examples of signs, that is, conventions that explicitly convey a message or denote some superficial aspect of reality, and whose appearance or even meaning can easily be changed by popular will. A symbol, however, such as a flag or a religious icon, has meaning beyond the specific thing it designates. In fact, a symbol almost by definition conveys more than can be explicitly explained and evokes emotional and physical responses to a wealth of connotative meanings. Thus, to many (especially those who have followed it into battle) the Stars and Stripes represent the suffering and sacrifice it took to destroy the Nazi and Japanese terror.

According to theologian Paul Tillich, a symbol is "transparent to" and "participates in" the reality to which it points. Unlike a sign, a symbol opens up levels of existential meaning and angst. Those who are "grasped by" the power of a flag, crucifix, menorah, Star of David, hammer and sickle, or other symbols are inwardly transformed. They may perform sacrificial and heroic deeds--or demonic ones. Obviously, symbols can be put to diabolic use. The Nazis employed the powerful symbolism of the Iron Cross, the swastika, and the myth of Aryan superiority to enlist Germans in the campaign to exterminate Jews and other non-Aryan populations.

Without knowing it, the students had attacked the symbolic foundation of Mulkern's life and that of my generation. Although they were students at a liberal arts college, they had not been liberated from narcissism and captivity to "the now." They seemed devoid of sensitivity and respect for generations other than their own. Revisionist historians had diminished or corroded the myths and the epics of splendor of American history. A slogan of the 60s--"Never trust anyone over 30"--had been taken as gospel. Such students were ignorant of the principle, "Never show disrespect to a symbol if you are *outside* its correlation of faith and value."

Symbols are created unconsciously when a nation undergoes a traumatic birthing experience. If the national loyalty and idealism expressed in those symbols is not regenerated and appropriated by each new generation, there is reason to believe that that civic community is *in extremis*. Symbols wither when they become opaque, empty, or "flat" and can no longer stimulate a community to heroism, sacrifice, and love. The Mulkerns of America consecrated themselves, not to a mere sign, but to the reality for which the American flag stands and out of which it came into being. Symbols die when they are no longer transparent to the ultimate concerns of the historical community that gave them birth.

In Canada the shift from the Union Jack to the Maple Leaf 40 years ago was a recognition that the English center was not holding. The banishment of the hammer and sickle over the Kremlin and its replacement with the Czarist Russian flag suggests that nationalistic centrifugal forces are more powerful than Marxist centripetal powers in the former Soviet Union. In America, what do the black, red, and green Afro-American flags that now hang in many inner city public schools portend for our future? Are we to see other rival symbols attesting to Latino, Asian, and other ethic loyalties that will destroy the *unum* in *e pluribus unum* "one out of many"?

During my tenure as an academic, I suspect some of my colleagues viewed Mulkern types as dinosaurs.

The walls of his office were covered with dozens of photos from his years in the Army Air Force. In contrast, many of his younger colleagues papered their walls with anti-military and anti-Vietnam slogans. It is sad, I believe, that neither they nor he ever got together to explore the values and loyalties inherent in their different symbols.

Despite the brief flurry of flags and yellow ribbons during Operation Desert Storm, a subtle anti-military ethos still pervades the campuses of many American colleges. Many colleges have eliminated ROTC programs and will not allow recruiters on campus because of the military position regarding homosexuals.

The last two World War II veterans on our faculty retired in 1994. A void now exists. No one is left to relate his personal and military journey during that war. For many ideologues and revisionist historians, the flag and the U.S. military still continue to generate negative sentiment. For too many, the nation and its military forces stand for sexism, genocide, racism, and imperialism. I believe, of course, the students are being short-changed. Nevertheless, if the flag is identified with only the nether side of the American experiment, tragically, a hopeful future for our posterity is certain to be foreclosed. I wonder, therefore, whether the flag will retain its symbolic power and be able to create a new legion of Mulkerns when our future survival may be at stake.

Hard Hat Teachers For A Day

When I joined the faculty of Hamline University in the fall of 1966, Dr. Joseph Uemura, Professor of Philosophy, and I were charged with creating an honors program. It was designed to increase intellectual stimulation for our best students. Our initiative, called the Presidential Scholarship program, involved weekly meetings of students who ranked in the top five percent of their high school classes. Each of our four classes was limited to 25 students, who did selected readings and created convocation programs for the academic community.

During the fall of 1971, our new library was under construction. The largest edifice on our campus, it's erection had been delayed briefly by a few who protested the cutting down of a few nondescript ash trees on the proposed site. After the trees were cut, a snow fence was installed to separate the site from the rest of the campus. I noticed that some of the burly workers would whistle at and make aesthetic judgments about our coeds as they walked by. Some of the young women seemed to enjoy nourishing the fantasy life of the workers amid their hazardous and difficult work.

The era was "B.P.C.," that is, "Before Political Correctness." Humor had not as yet been driven from college campuses. There was still a lot of good-natured joshing and sexual riposte among males and females. Male-bashing was still in its infancy. Radical feminists had not yet convinced their disciples that a rapist gene lay deep within the brain of every man, and that an appreciative whistle was grounds for filing a sexual harassment complaint.

As I watched the students and the workers over several days, I lamented the increasingly obvious fact that their two very different American worlds were passing like ships in the night on our campus. I wanted to see more than catcalls, sexual banter, and light-hearted give-and-take between them. But the snowfence that separated them could have been the Grand Canyon, indeed, the Berlin Wall, for all that our students and the workers knew about one another's world. The blue collar worker's world of hard knocks, which began at 7 a.m., stood in marked contrast to the privileged world of the students, who rarely chose a class that began before nine. I wondered whether those who carried a lunch bucket and those who shouldered a backpack had anything in common. I hoped so. Perhaps the future of our democracy depended upon it.

Moreover, I remembered Robert Frost's line, "There is something that does not like a wall." In educational jargon, I believed that a "teaching moment" was at hand. Students and journeyman workers occupied common Hamline turf. With the Vietnam war at fever pitch, I wanted these two classes of people to discover (and perhaps begin to understand and appreciate) each other's values.

As the mentor of the sophomore Presidential Scholars, I induced them to sponsor a convocation, "The Hardhat Philosophy of Life." I put on a flannel shirt, workboots, and a John Deere cap and climbed over the snow fence to issue the invitation. I told them, I too, had "worked" construction building log cabins in northern Minnesota. Yah, boy! They could spot a phony at 100 paces.

"Hey guys, it's pay-back time," I began. "Our cute coeds have been pleasuring your eyeballs. But we won't let you get by with only wolfish leers and catcalls." My attempt at humor struck out so I took another tack: "Seriously, on behalf of the faculty and students, we want to get to know you while you're on our campus." Three men in their 30s or 40s--a carpenter, a plumber, and an electrician--signed on to do our convocation. I think they felt sorry for me. But they worried, "What can we tell them?"

"Just be honest. They respect shooting straight," I pleaded. "Let the chips fall where they may. Don't try to be something you're not," I continued. "Give us a 'This Is Your Life' story and the students will respect you." It was a *pro bono* affair, a contract sealed by a round of handshakes. Their foremen gave them permission to leave the job site for no more than one hour.

On the day of the convocation the student center was packed with 600 students, faculty, and staff. I had alerted the press--they knew the story "had legs"--and they were there in force. I had recruited a fourth panelist, a member of the St. Paul Police Department. I wanted students to know at least one persona affected by the slogan, "Bust the Pigs!, directed against police officers during that era. The workers were dressed in clean and pressed blue jeans or tan khakis. They removed their hard hats and proudly placed them on the table by their names. Their clothes were in marked contrast to those of some of our students, who could easily have been mistaken for skid row denizens. Goodwill may not have accepted their duds as a donation!

The convocation was successful beyond my most fervent hope. The workers spoke with quiet dignity. One said he had attended college but had to drop out because of the death of his father. They spoke of having to leave their families for months at a time as they gypsy-skipped across America to work-sites in Alaska, Georgia, New Mexico, Montana, and Arizona. Like Native Americans following herds of Bison, our workers itinerated in synch with the construction cycle. Two had fought in Korea. One earned the Purple Heart as a result of a severe leg wound. Two of the three had retained their crew cuts, a cosmetic left-over from their military experience. Their command of English was surprisingly good, and they weren't cowed by the fact that this was probably the most awesome public speaking assignment in their lives. The four men bore little resemblance to the media's portrayal of the supposedly Neanderthal American worker as a knee-jerk, Archie Bunker-type reactionary.

Their ancestors had come from countries in Europe to "better themselves." I was reminded of Eric

Hoffer's notion that the common man has had a "romance with America" because here, in a land without caste, royalty, or the suffocating traditions of Europe, the greatness of ordinary people is allowed to flourish. The working men spoke of limited opportunities, the value of hard work, and the importance of home. Their wives were "nesters" who accepted and loved their role as homemakers.

Our workers religiously practiced the motto, "Buy American. Your Job Depends Upon It!" that was pasted on the bumpers of their pick-up trucks. All expressed anger that some bureaucrat was pushing minority hiring quotas for their trade thereby jeopardizing their sons' ability to follow in their footsteps. They expressed little envy that their kids might not be able to attend private liberal arts colleges that too often served the elite. The college dreams of "hardhat" offspring often had to be satisfied with a morning commute to a trade school or community college, followed by a rush to an afternoon and evening job.

The following are some random comments that I remember. It was as if these voices and messages came from another planet:

> For all of its faults, this is a good country. I was with the Marines in Korea. I know how the working man lives in other countries around the world. We are kings compared to them. I never finished high school, yet I own my own home and have two cars, a cabin and a boat in northern Minnesota. Get real, kids! This is the greatest country on earth
>
> I notice that some of you wear the flag on your butts. That makes me very angry. As far as I'm concerned, those of you who do that are piss-ing on my buddies who were killed in Korea. In the

military, we were told the flag should always be flown on a staff.

My son came home the other day and said that if his draft number came up, he was thinking of going to Canada. I pushed him up against the wall and said: "I fought for my country and you will too. I will not have a son with a yellow streak down his spine in this family." I think I convinced him that Americans have duties as well as rights.

Many people think union workers are over-paid. Listen! I was an apprentice for five years before getting my (journeyman) card. Sure, we make good money when we work. But some years when construction is down, we are laid off for three to six months.

I hope you people know how lucky you are. You have opportunities that I never had. I just hope that you make use of them and don't piss them away.

When the hour ended the students stood and applauded. Had a member of the faculty spoken like this, he would have been ridiculed. The hardhats conveyed personal integrity and decency. Their lives replicated their words. At the end of the day, they could see what they had accomplished. I suspect that I was among quite a few "word-smiths" who wondered about the falsity of much that passes for "mind culture." They belonged to the guild of "doers," whereas I was a member of the "chattering class."

But like most groups, our students had to have a scapegoat for their animus. I felt sorry for the policeman. In the students' minds, he toadied for their incarnation of evil, "the establishment," and was the focus of all of their hostile questions. Most of the queries put to him were of the genre, "When did you stop beating your wife?"

On the whole, however, I felt good about the session. Photos were taken of workmen and students talking together and coeds wearing the hardhats at a jaunty angle. Telephone numbers were shared so that the conversations could continue. Dates were made to break bread together. In Martin Buber's words, an authentic meeting, an epiphany of sorts, had taken place. People had shared a dialogue without pontificating about each others's righteousness and purity; ideology and stereotypes had been set aside for one precious hour.

I was sad when the library was completed. The hardhats moved on to continue doing their part to build a better America. And I worried that all too soon, our students might drift back again into their ideological cocoons.

A Poet Comes To Campus

According to Pat Conroy in Beach Music, the Vietnam War was the only foreign war ever to be fought on our own soil. Everyone was free to chose a side, but bystanders were ridiculed. Our entire country seemed to turn critically and self-consciously inward, and what had been old truisms were made to seem empty and antiquarian. In a matter of months our nation went from strutting self-confidence and bravado to craven self-doubt and national lunacy. While I considered the 60s to be silliest and stupidest of times, I recognized that Hamline's dementia was but a pale copy of its national counterpart. For the most part, we were lucky. The trauma on our campus, compared to other universities, was modest.

In the Fall of 1968, a prophet from the agrarian hinterland came to our turf and promised us enlightenment. His advance billing promised us a John the Baptist redivivus, one who would fire thunderbolts of judgment. Moreover, this Harvard-educated rural prophet professed to know the solutions to the enigmas in Washington and in Vietnam and all points in between. Alas, this prophet, unlike John the Baptist, did not leave his head on a platter but lived to spread his message. And while the original John dressed in the skins of wild animals and lived on honey and locusts, our modern prophet came for a fee. His presence was in great demand on American campuses. His thunderbolts and his love of mammon seemed inseparable.

The night Robert Bly spoke in our student union, he made "quite a splash," as one might say in the Land of 10,000 Lakes. His head stuck through a great cape of many colors, strings, and patches. It was difficult to tell whether it was supposed to replicate the garb of a Vatican official, a Native American chief, or a Greek Orthodox metropolitan. No matter. His wavy gray hair cascaded down over his shoulders.

He sat in utter repose as students and faculty crowded as close to the podium as possible. It seemed as if they wanted to be infused by his emanations. Bly sat Buddha-like, his face tilted upward at a 45 degree angle. He held the pose for close to 30 seconds after his introduction. His countenance seemed an admixture of Mona Lisa, Little Crow, and the war face of General George S. Patton, Jr. It was so quiet one could have heard a gnat hiccup. Bly, the bard, was psyching up, seemingly drawing strength from his muses, out of the ether. I was mesmerized before he spoke a word. He was playing his audience like a master musician plays his instrument.

Then he jumped up and stormed to the lectern. He threw his arms out wide and his verse gushed forth. He stomped back and forth, his voice ranging up and down the auditory keyboard. The medium was the message. I often lost his words in the posturing and prancing. Much of the poetry was beyond understanding or remembering. But his imagery was vivid if crude. "Consider that flesh," he shouted, "that Lyndon Johnson considers his face--a *stomach with eyes*." The students roared their approval. It was a good show. Bly was a secularized Billy Sunday or an Elmer Gantry who could hold a crowd without pounding the Good Book.

So far it was all good fun, a campus catharsis. Shout fortissimo what radical profs are saying pianissimo across the land. Preen and posture, shout, sing, and sway. The times are too serious to emote at athletic contests. Besides, revivals come in different forms. I, too, was beginning to enjoy the show, a communal gushing.

Then Bly did the unpardonable. When asked by students "what can we do?" he responded, "*get to the president.*" Egged on by Bly, they poured out of the student center and mob-marched to the home of Hamline's president, which, ironically, is known as the "White House." Several students pulled the hinge pins out of the front door, took it off, and the cold night air streamed into the house. Student self-righteousness didn't respect the Anglo-Saxon principle, "A man's home is his castle." When President Richard Bailey finally appeared, the students demanded he leave immediately for Washington and "stop this 'freaking' war!"

Bailey was the answer to Hamline's dreams and needs. Known as a "builder president," our new president was a master at playing catch-up regarding our woefully inadequate physical plant. In earlier years, as the innovative president of a community college, he had been honored by President Johnson. A photo of the two of them rested proudly on his desk. On the basis of that 30-second, oval office photo-op, the protesting students foolishly concluded that Bailey had the leverage to help "end the war." Bly stood in the shadows and smiled. Bailey got his door back only after promising to go to Washington. "This is a futile gesture" was his parting shot to them.

Today the Hamline president lives 12 miles from campus in private housing. The school's White House is only used to entertain potential donors.

After the war in Vietnam ended, Bly discovered other poetic niches. He compromised his academic and feminist credibility by writing a best seller--*Iron John*-- that sought the empowerment of angry white males. His hair is now white and closely trimmed. In place of his splendiferous cape, he regularly appears in shirts, ties and sport coats. His finger is ever on our cultural pulse. Chameleon-like, he knows there is a conservative tide. His poetry is now in sync with the new anger that stalks our land.

Twenty-five years ago he empowered dissolute students. Now he helps men plumb their souls for Iron John, the patrician mentor they never knew. Bly has become the shaman-healer for white males, who are now stereotyped as the victimizers of all other groups in America. Hated by feminists, despised by their children, dumped on by their wives, made redundant by corporations, and labeled racist by racial minorities, the present white male and his psyche are in sad shape. Bly's new shtick has a market potential many times greater than the one he discovered on college campuses. He shows his wounded males how to get in touch with their child-self via the Great Bunyanesque Father of ancient texts and Jungian psychology.

Bly's disciples do primal screams, beat their chests and drums, and run like children in their forest retreats. They dress up like the wild-men, cry and hug a lot, bond, purge, and spill their guts to their fellow sufferers in front of evening campfires. It is a religious ritual without conventional and traditional sacral symbols. The truth-seekers find out where it all went wrong--too many women in their lives, too much law, too little grace, absent male mentors who should have been like the native Israeli sabra--hard on the outside, tender on the inside. Almost too late, they try to make up for a fractured childhood and adolescence. Is this all a con job, a new form of psychobabble? In the regions of the soul, proof is impossible.

I surmise that Bly's royalties and engagement fees have skyrocketed. While he continues to damn market capitalism, he seems to know every weather-vane shift of the market. His poetry is now that of the establishment. He might even be capable of teaching Entrepreneurship 201 or Marketing 101 at Hamline. That is, if no one remembers the wounds he left there in the late 1960s.

Twelve

Is The Warrior A Barbarian?

> I have a rendezvous with Death
> On some scarred slope of battered hill,
> When Spring comes round again this year
> And the first meadow-flowers appear.
>
> God knows 'twere better to be deep
> pillowed in silk and scented down,
> Where love throbs out in blissful sleep,
> Pulse nigh to pulse, and breath to breath,
> Where hushed awakenings are dear . . .
> But I've a rendezvous with Death
> At midnight in some flaming town,
> When Spring trips north again this year,
> And I to my pledged word am true,
> *I shall not fail that rendezvous.*

Harvard graduate and poet, Alan Seeger, a member of the French Foreign Legion, penned the above poem, *Rendezvous*, shortly before his death in 1916. Nothing like it, either in tone or in substance came from our warriors during their decade of engagement in Southeast Asia. For, unlike the two World Wars and the Korean conflict, the Vietnam experience irrevocably sullied for millions the very idea that soldiering can be a noble vocation. Sailor, soldier, airman, marine, all now belong to a Gnostic realm of darkness from which redemption is impossible and a humane existence is excluded. Military righteousness is impossible in the post-Vietnam two-world cosmology, for a good/evil, light/darkness, civilian/military, pacifist/militarist dualism prevents it. To enter the military is to be swallowed up in a modern heart of darkness experience so graphically portrayed in such films as *Apocalypse Now* and *The Deer Hunter*.

This remains true, I believe, in spite of the momentary "high" the nation and its military forces experienced as a result of Operation Desert Storm in 1990. The media elite, the Protestant mainline, the press, and the intellectual and academic communities were almost lock-step solid against President Bush's courageous stand. Their view was especially difficult to comprehend because the United Nations sanctioned our initiative, many Arab countries sent troops, and Sadam Hussein was seen as the pariah of the world.

In comparison to the 20 million Americans who served in the war against Germany and Japan, only 500,000 soldiers were involved in Desert Storm. Largely drawn from minority groups and the working class, they spent only a few months in the arid landscape. The omnipresent campus signs, "No Blood For Oil," spoke for our disenchanted elites who refused to believe that Kuwait may have been the Belgium of 1914 or the Austria, Czechoslovakia, or Poland of 1939. In sum, for too many, soldiers are still baby-killers and barbarians. The rhetoric of the 60's was recycled in the 90's.

Unlike most European countries where the military is firmly rooted in a proud and illustrious past, there is a strain of the American ethos that is still hostile to the warrior. But the warrior-soldier-defender-as-barbarian is a created image, not a norm. To regard the soldier as either below or beyond human sensibilities, either bestial or demonic, violates Scripture. Jesus' harshest condemnations fell upon professional clergy (Pharisees) and professional lawyers (scribes), not on the professional military. In healing the son of a Roman centurion, Jesus declared this soldier's faith unique in all of Israel. At the foot of the cross, another centurion declared Jesus innocent and praised God. Moreover, if the vocation of the soldier was wholly beyond the pale, would Paul, in his letter to the Ephesians, have used the armor of the Roman legionnaire as a metaphor in describing the struggle to keep the Christian faith alive in the world?

The image of the soldier as a barbarian also runs counter to the Protestant doctrine of vocation. In repudiating the Greek-medieval dichotomy between higher and lower forms of work, Luther affirmed that it was the spirit of the work, not its nature, that made a vocation Christian. Like their civilian counterparts, the police and most military persons are motivated by altruistic ideals, e.g., the restraint of evil and the protection of the defenseless.

A contemporary hymn wisely includes the warrior as a "saint of God" whose vicarious sacrifice is the incarnation of agape. Priest and soldier alike fight "wild beasts," albeit with different weapons:

> I sing a song of the saints of God, patient and brave and true,
> Who toiled and fought and lived and died for the Lord they loved and knew,
> And one was a doctor, and one was a queen, and one was a shepherdess on the green;
> They were all of them saints of God, and I mean, God helping, to be one too.
>
> They loved their Lord so dear, so dear, and his love made them strong;

And they followed the right for Jesus' sake the
whole of their good lives long.
And one was a soldier, and one was a priest,
and one was slain by a fierce wild beast;
And there's not any reason, no, not the least,
why I shouldn't be one too.

The image of the soldier as a barbarian also is at odds with the Western literary tradition. If the warrior is a vocational leper, how can one teach or appreciate the heroism of Achilles and Hector in *The Iliad*? What is one to make of Plato's giving the guardians a central role in *The Republic*? If the calling of the soldier is indelibly vitiated, can one ever again appreciate classics, such as *The Red Badge of Courage*, that dramatize the struggle for moral courage? And how is one to regard countless others, great and small, famous and obscure, who were at once military leaders and sensitive human beings: Joan of Arc, George Washington, Lord Nelson, Andrew Jackson, Robert E. Lee, George Marshall, Dwight Eisenhower, and Colin Powell? Even Pope John Paul II served for a time in the Polish army.

A professional soldier understands that war may require killing people, war nearly always involves maiming people, and war leaves families without fathers and sons. "All you have to do is hold your first dying soldier in your arms," reflected General Norman Schwarzkopf, "and have that terribly futile feeling that his life is flowing out and you can't do anything about it. Then you understand the horror of war." That was Schwarzkopf's experience in Vietnam and he never forgot it.

General George S. Patton loved the opportunity that war presented to use the skill, leadership, and courage that his calling required, much as a surgeon loves his profession but not the disease, illness, and injury he fights. Warriors worth their salt should be antiwar. Yet, they know that there are values worth fighting for and a dimension of freedom that transcends life and death. For warriors the abstract concepts of duty, patriotism, honor, and glory are more than the platitudes of Memorial Day speeches. They are the controlling and living values that shape the warrior persona. Bravery is the highest virtue, cowardice the deadliest sin.

The image of warriors as barbarians allows us to exclude them from the realm of moral discourse, to cast them in the role of outsider. Those who do this, and I think particularly of some clergy, media elite, and academicians, need to reexamine their views. It is better, as Kipling wrote of his Tommy Atkins, to view warriors as neither saints "nor black- guards too/But single men in barracks most remarkable like you."

During the dismal years of the 1920s, when the U.S. maintained a skeleton military force only slightly more than 100,000 men, Dwight Eisenhower and George Patton recalled seeing signs in communities near army posts saying, *"Dogs and Soldiers Keep Off the Grass"* Douglas MacArthur, according to William Manchester in *American Caesar*, believed that decade was a spiritual desert for the professional soldier. It was the era of Kellogg-Briand, meager military budgets, obsolete weapons, and unglamourous rescue missions amid floods and mining accidents. Only twelve postwar tanks were in service during that period. Yet, when the military chiefs pointed out war clouds on the horizon, they were labeled as warmongers. In one of his many hat-in-hand sojourns before Congress, MacArthur was humiliated: Manchester reports:

> When one congressman, noting the army's budget for toilet paper, asked him with heavy irony, "General, do you expect a serious epidemic of dysentery in the U.S.Army?" MacArthur rose. "I

have humiliated myself," he said bitterly. "I have licked the boots of some gentlemen to get funds for the motorization and mechanization of the army. Now, gentlemen, you have insulted me. I am as high in my profession as you are in yours. When you are ready to apologize, I shall be back."

We can be grateful that dedicated senior officers such as Pershing, MacArthur and Summerall and junior officers such as Marshall, Eisenhower and Patton stuck it out despite numerous disincentives--appalling living conditions, miserable pay, public disdain for their calling--and no apparent incentives at all to remain soldiers. Some had generous offers from Wall Street and American corporations (J. P. Morgan and Company approached Douglas MacArthur). But against conventional common sense, they stayed and endured the years of the locust. The outcome of World War II might have been different had they not done so.

Thirteen

The Enduring Appeal Of War

I do not know what is true. I do not know the meaning of the universe. But in the midst of doubt, in the collapse of creeds, there is one thing I do not doubt, that no man who lives in the same world with most of us can doubt, and that is that the faith is true and adorable which leads a soldier to throw away his life in obedience to a blindly accepted duty, in a cause which he little understands, in a plan of campaign of which he has no notion, under tactics of which he does not see the use.

These words were written by Oliver Wendell Holmes, Jr., a mature man of 54 and a veteran of the Civil War. They seem at odds with our time, when there is a growing unwillingness to glorify war and the military virtues. In modern literature, authors are unlikely to depict (much less justify) war in terms of the heroic deeds it calls forth, or to romanticize its grandeur, or to exalt its personal sacrifices.

Nonetheless, *Homo sapiens*, for all of his assumed rationality, is a *homo furens*, a fighting man. There is a strange dichotomy and conflictedness in our nature.

"Since the dawn of time," according to Carolo D'Este, "men have been driven by an unfathomable need to prove their courage and masculinity in some bizarre rite of passage that defines their lives."

But isn't the notion of giving up one's life in a foreign land both frightening as well as repugnant? Of course it is. Yet, strangely enough, we both fear and are attracted by the monstrous cruelty of war. Siegfried Sassoon, the great British poet of World War I, wrote "Soldiers are dreamers;/ when the guns begin/ They think of firelit homes, clean beds, and wives." In spite of the dwindling martial spirit among 20th century writers, war will always have a deadly fascination.

J. Glenn Gray states in *The Warriors: Reflections On Men In Battle*, that war is a delight to the eye. Anyone who has come across an accident on the highway with people crowding around has experienced what the Bible calls "the lust of the eye." While I experienced my share of boredom in the Navy, there were epiphanies of wonder. Thousands of warriors marching in unison and graced by bands, flags, tanks, artillery pieces and other weapons of war, are an awesome spectacle to behold. The Pipestone parades celebrating the Fourth of July were only three blocks long and were laughable in comparison. When our Privateers flew in close formation and we let go with a stick of practice bombs, all eyes turned in unison to see the effect on the target. When we let go with our 50-calibers guns on sleeves and sea sleds, the sight and sound was exhilarating. I wanted more.

Those who spend their careers in academe tend to judge that the sights of battle are overwhelmingly ugly and that aesthetic delight must be limited to subjects such as the Mona Lisa, Winged Victory, butterflies, mountain ranges, and sunsets. Not so. The color and movement, power and proportion, harmony and energy of a collectivity of men, ships or tanks that move as one

The Enduring Appeal Of War 137

is addictive to the eye. An armada of any kind is overwhelming to the senses. Long after he became disillusioned with the Vietnam War, Philip Caputo would still remember the eight-inch batteries of self-propelled howitzers pounding out landing zones in the mountains:

> Tongues of flame flicked from the long, black barrels. The shells went hissing overhead. The Cordillera beautiful in the clear air . . .golden-green high up . .greenish-black lower down . . . helicopters rising into the clean sky . . . explosions echoed and reechoed through the mountains . . Gray puffs of smoke . . . Mists curling up through the jungle. *The scene charmed me.*

Warriors report an ecstatic feeling on such occasions, a *mysterium tremendum*, which is not unlike a religious experience. Though he had been severely wounded only two months earlier, George Patton wrote of the Armistice ending World War I, "Well this is a hellish stupid world now and *life has lost its zest.*" A few miles away, Captain Harry S. Truman was both elated and relieved that he had survived the war: he remarked later that combat had been "the most terrific experience of my life." This eye-gate alternation between the attraction and revulsion of war seems universal. It was the sight of advancing columns of men under fire that prompted General Robert E. Lee to remark, "It is well that war is so terrible--we would grow too fond of it."

After a successful firefight in Vietnam in which his platoon had performed to perfection, Lieutenant Philip Caputo "felt a drunken elation. When the line wheeled and charged across the clearing, the enemy bullets whining past them, wheeled and charged almost with drill-field precision, an ache as profound as the ache of orgasm passed through me." Perhaps the longing to experience this ecstasy is the reason why some officers make careers in the military and submit to years of ridiculous regulations, discomforts, degradations, and dreary posts. Commanders hunger for a form of rapture where, in the stress of combat, men obey their will and become an extension of themselves. Civilian equivalents, perhaps, are the experiences of the orchestra conductor or the corporate CEO.

But with peace, adjustment comes hard; the "high" of combat is over, and only the stories, myths, and psychic hangover remain. In battle warriors are often granted perceptions that are forever denied to civilians. These perceptions are the raw material out of which both great novels and terrifying nightmares arise. The wonder and terror of such events as D-Day (*The Longest Day*), when 5,000 ships stood off the Normandy coast and wave after wave of planes swept overhead, may never be seen again. The impressions of such epic battles, from Hastings in 1066 A.D. to Picket's charge at Gettysburg, are forever etched in man's collective memory. The impacts of classic struggles--Troy, Waterloo, Verdun, Somme, Stalingrad, El Alamein, the Battle of the Bulge, Berlin, and Desert Storm and more--were so awesome that they were engraved indelibly in the memories of the participants and in the pictures and pages of history.

I corresponded with one of my crewmates some 20 years after we served together. Life had not gone well for him. Severely depressed, he looked back to our time in the squadron with nostalgia. "Anything is better than my life and my boring routine at present. I do not wish for war, Heaven forbid. But I have not felt as alive as I did when we were training together in our squadron."

The eye also delights in destruction. Who has not seen children pile blocks on top of each other, only to scream with delight when they are knocked down? As a child I enjoyed firecrackers on the Fourth of July. I put them in the cracks of trees, in tin cans, in the sand box, and in anything else I could think of that would show their destructive force. Most of the observers of the Indianapolis 500 are eager to see a smash-up of race cars (so long as no one is injured). The destruction of a building by a wrecking ball or by implosion will attract a crowd. War holds the same fascination, though the extent of the destruction is multiplied a thousand-fold.

Military rituals, like religious ceremonies, can be highly attractive to both eye and spirit. Carlo D'Este cites memories of the funerals held at Arlington National Cemetery during the inter-war years, as recounted by General Patton's daughter, Ruth Ellen:

> We were all used to the sound of the Dead March, booming out three or four times a day-- and oftener during the flu season. Once Ma found sister Bee and me dancing solemnly behind the tombstones to the hymn, "Abide With Me." There was something basic and terrible and splendid about the flag-draped coffin on the caisson . . . the curveting charger with the rider's empty boots turned backwards in the stirrups (to confuse the ghost, Pa told us) led by a soldier, who in the olden times, would have been sacrificed on the tomb so that he could join his dead master. The terrible throb of the music reached us as nothing else ever had--I know now that it was like the sound of irreconcilable grief.

Upon returning home, many warriors are uncomfortable about being asked what combat was like. Many evade answering honestly, lest they be labeled war-lovers. "The truth is," Philip Caputo confessed, "I felt happy. The nervousness had left me the moment I got into the helicopter, and I felt happier than I ever had. I don't know why." Poets can warn about the horror of war's slaughter, but Ares, the Greek god of war and Pied Piper to young men, seems to lead them irresistibly to that unique frontier between life and death. Each generation, it seems, is condemned to fight its own war, confront the same experiences, face the loss of the same cherished illusions, and master the same lessons on its own. "The greatest tragedy is war," reflects Jomini in *The Art of War*, "but so long as there is mankind, there will be war."

Fourteen

Love: War's Ally and Foe

The Greeks were wise when they mated Ares, the god of war, with the goddess of love, Aphrodite. The two of them spent many sweet, albeit illicit, hours together. In *The Warriors*, Glenn Gray wondered how it is possible that these two seemingly contradictory human propensities--killing and love-making--can have such an attraction for each other? Anyone who has been in the military remembers his comrades' intense interest in women and, more specifically, the fixation on the sex act. The overuse of the vulgar expression for sexual intercourse--which serves as adjective, adverb, verb and noun in both positive and negative, even hostile, contexts--seems to reveal the strange polarity of attraction and repulsion regarding love and killing.

For uniformed warriors, there is a strong erotic attraction to almost any woman who seems the least bit attractive. Strangely enough, the interest is often reciprocated. Legions of women have a notorious interest in, if not passion for, men in uniform, especially during wartime. When I marched in close order drill down the streets of Memphis, I heard teen aged girls giggle with delight and scream, "There's a cute one . . . he's mine! . . . Sally, you can have that one with the red curly hair." Carefully nurtured canons of chastity and inhibition are often lowered simply by a chance meeting with a soldier on the street or during a wartime dance. Mysteriously, war seems to increase the passions between the sexes that result in an increase of marriage and birth.

Sociological and biological explanations of this phenomenon are helpful, although they are not entirely satisfactory. Advocates for the former point to the uprootedness, isolation, and loneliness that wartime produces. Heightened erotic interest may be a compensatory form of adjustment, an expression of a search for belonging amid social dislocation. Strange environments result in abnormal behaviors.

Biological psychologists affirm an evolutionary, deterministic theory to account for the intensified interest in sex during wartime. By killing off the fit along with the unfit, they argue, war threatens our survival as a species. Thus, this theory holds that the acceleration of copulation during war is simply a Darwinian, naturalistic-survivalist response to wholesale slaughter. Driven by a compensatory genetic impulse, we have no freedom in the matter.

While such explanations have some plausibility, they cannot stand alone. Love is more than an imperative arising from the loins. It is a mysterious reality, a uniquely human spiritual quality as well as a biological act. In the Greek language, love has more nuances than in English and can be rendered as *Eros*, *Storge*, *Philia*, and *Agape*.

As *Eros*, love is equated with sexual passion; it is a natural act that fulfills biological needs, like eating and drinking. At its best, erotic love seeks fulfillment without harm to its object. But it can also seek gratification without regard for the other's well-being, e.g. through employment of a prostitute. Erotic gratification in a rawer and darker form exists where a warrior "devours" the women as an object. The famous

Renaissance painting, "The Rape of the Sabine Women" depicts a perversion of eros that, tragically enough, has been re-enacted upon the women of the vanquished by the victors in virtually every war ever fought. Before the Battle of Berlin, Russian officers stood by as their soldiers ravished tens of thousands of German women. It was pay-back time--a deliverance of eye-for-an-eye justice--for the monstrous horrors of plunder and pillage that the German SS had wrought on Slavic women and property. In China, Japanese invaders perpetrated the infamous "Rape of Nanking," in which 200,000 Chinese were raped, tortured, and killed.

According to St. Augustine, the nuns of Rome who were ravished by Visigoth invaders, nevertheless retained their chastity because they had not consented to their violation. Chastity is a product of the intention and determination of one's will, not of physical condition. In such cases, women are not destroyed but only momentarily overthrown. To talk about "making love" in association with rape is a horror, because such copulation is an act of aggression, power, and vengeance that has nothing to do with love--and little to do with sex.

But there is often a higher eroticism in the warrior. Soldiers are often starved for the qualities of gentleness and affection that women manifest. Feminists are mistaken if they assume that the hundreds of cheesecake, pin-up photos of women that adorned our barracks were regarded by us only as sex objects. However attractive and curvaceous, those photos were mediators of a beauty, softness, and nurture that I knew I did not possess. In my lonely and isolated masculine world, I hungered for the gentleness, texture, and caring that is uniquely feminine. I was not alone in that search for a higher eroticism.

Women were the angels, light, and warmth in a Yin-Yang equation of human nature. They mediated the softer side of our "humanness" that is at risk during war. I did not believe then, nor do I believe now, that both genders can be collapsed into a unisex uniformity. There are gender-specific qualities that each sex needs from the other to be complete. Confronted daily by a violent and rigid world, warriors long for the healing that comes not only from a woman's body, but, from her touch, gentleness, voice, sensitivity, indeed, her inner presence.

In 1944, in thousands of liberated towns across France, Belgium, and Holland, young women who had genuinely fallen in love with German soldiers had their heads shaved. Some were driven naked through gauntlets of screaming partisans. Members of the underground could not understand how "their women" could have had sexual relations with the enemy. But higher eroticism is not bounded by nationalistic limits. It is a cosmic, ecstatic, and uncontrollable blessing that occasionally brought couples together, even if momentarily, in the chaos of war.

Storge, as "family affection," refers to a form of love that has little application in combat. The civilians in the dozens of countries ravaged by the wars of the twentieth century, however, existentially experienced the meaning of the phrase, "blood is thicker than water." They had to share food, clothing and housing. This form of love turns a family from hedonistic self-indulgence to caring for each other. It can occur not only in wartime but during times of unemployment, natural catastrophe, divorce, and the death of loved ones. As a natural form of love, it may not be as heroic as other forms; even felons are benevolent and sacrificial in behalf of their children.

Philia: This form of love is defined as "friendship" or "brotherly-love." Warriors do not have to like each other, but "they must have an overwhelming *concern* for one another." Our plane crew was very diverse. Strange as it may seem, I did not like many of my Navy comrades. Nevertheless, I had to love them, i.e., I had to show them benevolence and be willing to sacrifice for them if need be. One of the military police I patrolled with on the Northern Pacific bedded hundreds of women during his stint in the service. With great elan and verve he enjoyed telling me about his exploits. Outwardly, he and I performed a common task of military control, but our values were completely different.

This sergeant was a comrade, not a friend. Glenn Gray believes that erotic lovers and comrades often lose their identities, while friends expand their self-awareness and individuality. I had very little in common with that sergeant. Only those warriors who can be friends possess an intellectual and emotional affinity with each other. Erotic love can usually find another partner when a lover departs but the loss of a companion-friend on the battlefield is irreplaceable.

Agape is an ultimate concern for the neighbor, the sacrificial gift of the self to the other. Napoleon once said that he could make men die for a little piece of ribbon. Perhaps so, but most warriors die for the love of their comrades. "Greater love hath no man, than he lays down his life for his friend." *Agape* is a form of preservative love that keeps the soul intact even in the most barbaric of conditions. When a warrior knows that his comrade-friend is willing to lay down his life for him, combat may lose part of its terror. An *agape*-bond between soldiers is a powerful antidote to the feelings of nihilism, impotence, and helplessness that exist during combat.

The communion between warriors is as profound as any between lovers, perhaps more so. It does not require for its continuance the reciprocity, the pledges of affection, the endless reassurances required by the lovers. It is unlike marriage, according to Philip Caputo in *A Rumor of War*; it is a bond that cannot be broken by a word, by boredom or divorce, or by anything other than death. Sometimes even death is not strong enough, as men die trying to retrieve the corpses of their fallen comrades from the battlefield. Amid the barbarism of conflict, *agape* is the one divine and ennobling sentiment of its participants.

It is easy to see why a group of terrorists would never attempt to highjack a plane full of soldiers. The bonding process in the training of the warrior severely leaches out self-regard. Thus, a platoon becomes a collective, an organic whole. Thoughts and reactions become intuitive and automatic. Whereas a group of civilians would most likely be traumatized and unable to coordinate the moves needed to recapture the aircraft, the soldiers would overthrow the terrorists by a coordinated movement--a wink, sign, gesture, feint, thrust, repulse, attack--that arose from an *agape* bond. Risk, sacrifice, and safety are jointly shared.

Agape can sometimes induce a soldier to redefine "friendship" and make sacrifices for persons other than his comrades-in-arms. During the occupation of Holland, a member of a German firing squad refused to shoot an innocent Dutch hostage. After refusing several commands to aim his weapon, he was blindfolded and shot with the hostage minutes later. While during wartime the bond of *agape* helps insulate us from being delivered entirely over to the forces of nihilism and destruction, it is easy to see that the true domain of *agape*-love can only be peace.

Fifteen

The Military As Family

For many professional warriors, the military is the only real community they have ever known. For them it is a fellowship deeper than any they have experienced, either in their families or churches. Their backgrounds rarely include a lovely suburban family with station wagon and black Labrador, a family that alternately skis in Colorado and "browns" in Bermuda, whose children are heir to the best orthodontists, summer camps, and Ivy League schools that money and status can buy. Instead, the histories of many professional soldiers, or "lifers," reveal fathers who brutalized, mothers who deserted, and placements in foster homes and orphanages. The protagonist of *An Officer and a Gentleman*, Zach Mayo, having been pushed to super-human limits and urged to drop out of officer training school by Foley, his black drill instructor, screams, "I have *no other place to go!*" As Mayo's D.I., Foley is the substitute father that he had never had. Foley and Mayo--each in his own way an outsider--come to respect each other in military "brotherhood."

Tragically, fatherless wastelands exist in our vast urban areas. Threatened by increased poverty, illegitimacy, drugs, crime, and gangs, our social cohesion is fraying. Millions of underclass mothers are raising underclass children, sheltered by public housing projects, fed by food stamps, doctored by Medicaid, taught by Head Start, Title 1 GED, and job-training programs. Usually to no avail. In a classic example of the Law of Unintended Consequences, states David Popenone, "the family under the welfare state is gradually losing both the ability and the will to care for itself." The military certainly cannot totally replace the two-parent family, but it has served and is serving as a positive family substitute for many ghetto youth who have entered its ranks.

Outside the marital bond, the covenants that link us with other members of *Homo sapiens* are often fragile, temporary, and superficial. They are often based on ego needs and a drive for personal success. We shuffle in and out of many of these associations as easily as we change seasonal wardrobes. The bond between warriors, on the other hand, like that which unites the police, is existential and involves issues of life and death. Compared to the bonds of steel that link warriors, some of our civilian linkages seem like rubber bands.

In the military the squad, platoon, and company loom larger than the ego. Training assumes that comrades may have to defend each other in conflict. Thus the bonding process is immediate and intense: begun in fear, it intensifies as common sacrifices, challenges, and goals are met.

"We belong to a group not only because we are born into it, not merely because we profess to belong to it, nor finally because we give it our loyalty and allegiance, but primarily because we see the world the way it does," states Karl Mannheim in *Ideology and Utopia*. "In every concept, in every concrete meaning, there is contained a crystallization of the experiences of a certain group." In most cases it's not some grand ideological cause that propels soldiers into battle, but rather their sense of oneness with their comrades, who have become a surrogate family.

In *War and Rumor of War*, Roger Shinn states that combat requires and builds trust. Men who read the fine print before signing purchase orders, who hire lawyers to draw up foolproof contracts on trivial issues, who bargain incessantly over the price of a new car, change completely in combat. They make instantaneous commitments: "You cover me while I make a move, then I'll cover you." A soldier may say that to someone he knows to be a cheater at cards (though usually outside his squad), a seducer of women, a drunkard when on liberty, and a chiseler on his income tax. But in combat, the two count on their mutual trust in an instantaneous and unenforceable agreement concerning life and death.

"I used to look upon those in uniform with disdain," reflected a newly commissioned officer who had been a campus radical in the 1960s. "No longer. I now know the rigor of training they went through." "In those wandering first weeks after the return," a veteran confessed to Shinn, "I perceived that the only time in my life I had had an identity other than my vague personal goals had been as a member of a combat unit in Vietnam." In James Webb's novel, *A Sense of Honor*, Lenahan, a Vietnam veteran, reflects: "So who wants to get out? No, it's what I always wanted to do, lead troops. Civilian life? Fifty grand a year, a company car, two martinis at lunch, and then what? I love the military, Maria, all the way down to my nerve-damaged toes."

W.E.B. Griffin, the contemporary novelist and former Marine, is described by Tom Clancy as "the best man around for describing the military community." All of his 20 novels are best-sellers and together have sold over 18 million copies. Grouped under the three categories of "Brotherhood of War," "The Corps," and "Badge of Honor," his epics uniquely describe what goes on in the hearts and minds of those who, by choice or circumstance, are called upon to fight our nation's wars.

Colin Powell discovered that the military embodies the democratic ideal far more so than the rest of America. "Beginning in the 50s, less discrimination, a truer merit system, and leveler playing fields existed inside the gates of our military posts than in any southern city hall or northern corporation," he wrote in *My American Journey*. Whatever its flaws, the Army made it easier for Powell "to love my country and to serve her with all my heart."

As military sophistication increases, some futurists predict that machines will overcome and surpass the human element in war. That was a position with which General George S. Patton never agreed: In *Patton: A Genius for War*, Carolo D'Este, cites a tactics paper written in 1933:

> When Samson took the fresh jawbone of an ass and slew a thousand men therewith he probably started such a vogue for the weapon . . . that for years no prudent donkey dared to bray. History is replete with countless other instances of military implements, each in its day heralded as the last word--the key to victory--yet each in its turn subsiding to its useful but inconspicuous niche. Today machines hold the place formerly occupied by the jawbone, the elephant, armor, the longbow, gun powder, and latterly, the submarine. *They too shall pass.*

Those who despise the military culture may ridicule the antics of members of the American Legion and the Veterans of Foreign Wars. What with their parades, beer bellies, bingo parties, raffles, war stories, and a jingoism that is often spiced with an antediluvian conservatism, there are plenty of reasons to hold many veterans in derision. Indeed, their behavior sometimes seems hopelessly out of synch with the American values they profess to hold dear. Those who scorn, however, might do well to peer beneath the surface of such frolic. There they might find bonds based on some past defining moment in the shaping of personal identity, where egoistic need was subordinated to the service of country.

The narcotic-like effect of military bonding is so powerful that even a successful family life or material success cannot be an adequate substitute. Carlo D'Este believes that the end of war produces a culture shock that often results in alcoholism and depression. Warriors honed to a keen edge cannot be expected to become instant pillars of society.

Though the military in many ways does become a substitute family, many families are dysfunctional; perhaps, therefore, the more apt psychic metaphor for the military is the monastery. Both the warrior and the monastic have an existence that is geographically "within" but psychologically "outside" the world. Under both military and monastic rules there is discipline, harmony, and belonging. Both involve common hours, uniforms, meals, duties, dogmas, and rituals. In both institutions the "we" looms larger than the "I." Both have symbols and ceremonies that honor founders, martyrs, and past heroic moments that define their existence as separate from the larger world.

In many ways the fence surrounding a military base is analogous to the walls of a monastery. To leave the confines of either is to enter another world, one in which disrespect for law and libertarianism reign. The traffickers of mammon abound and hedonistic slogans assault one's sensibilities: "Grab all the gusto you can," "Enjoy, Enjoy," "You only go around once," "If you've got it, flaunt it," "You owe it to yourself." Avarice, gluttony, and licentiousness abound. On base one can scarcely find a discarded cigarette butt or candy wrapper, but in Vanity Fair both gutter and billboard testify to the insatiable appetites of sensate life. If the military *civitas* is Sparta, the secular *civitas* looks suspiciously like Sodom.

The ritual closing each day in a monastery is compline or evensong, the last of the seven daily offices of the Benedictine *Rule*. The military parallel is the bugler sounding taps, as activity ceases and the American flag is reverently lowered and folded and retired until reveille the next morning. "The squad of marines walked slowly and in single file, heads down, hooded ponchos billowing in the wind," observed Philip Caputo. The stocks of their rifles, slung muzzle-down against the rain, bulged under the backs of the ponchos. Caputo was amazed--the marines, hooded and bowed, "resembled a column of hunchbacked, penitent monks."

The mutuality of military comradeship stands in sharp contrast to the hedonism of civilian competitiveness. With few exceptions honor codes work in the military academies. They seldom do in academia, even in elitist Ivy League colleges. In this age of egoism and self-centeredness, we often form quite fragile and tentative alliances with schools, corporations, and even our spouses in pursuit of individual success and emotional satisfaction. Novelist Tom Wolfe described the 1970s as the "Me decade." Christopher Lasch labeled the 1980s a "culture of narcissism." The renowned sociologist and communitarian, Amitai Etzioni, in reviewing much of the same data, sees a "hollowing of America" and laments the concern for "number one" that is crippling basic American institutions.

There are few things in life more satisfying than to be accepted as an equal in a fraternity of fighting men. Everyone is a full member in an aristocracy of merit. "We Marines are all in this together," says Flap, an aircraft carrier pilot in Steven Coont's *The Intruders*:

When one man slips off the rope, we'll grab him on the way down. We'll all hang together and we'll do what we have to do to get the job done. The Corps is bigger than all of us, and once you are part of it, you are part of it together. *Semper Fidelis.* If you die, when you die, the Corps goes on. *It's sorta like the church.*

When the protagonist, Lt. Jake Grafton, suggests to his commander that he is thinking of leaving the military to fly for the airlines, Colonel Haldane responds:

Pretty boring, if you ask me. Take off from point A and fly to point B. Land. Taxi to the gate. Spend the night in a motel. The next day fly back to A. I think a man of your training and experience would go quietly nuts doing something like that. You'd be a glorified bus driver.
"Civilians' worlds are too small," adds Warrant Officer Muldowski. "They get a job, live in a neighborhood, shop in the same stores all their lives. They live in a little world of friends, work, family. Those worlds look too small to me."

However strong the fraternal bond among members of the warrior guild, their lives differ from those of most monastics or civilians in that they are not allowed to become deeply rooted in any particular geographic space. Military families are nomads and gypsies, worldwide migratory folk whose families drift in and out of schools, communities, and churches. Military housing is often colorless, with less character and poorer upkeep than the student apartments of a mediocre community college. "Military brats" often testify to a sense of alienation. They resist getting close to their school-age peers because they are only passing through. Military families often enter and leave a community unnoticed and unpraised. In *Leaves From the Notebooks of a Tamed Cynic*, Reinhold Niebuhr recounts meeting a salesman on a train who, upon seeing two nuns in habit, felt very superior and asked, "How can anyone fall for that stuff?" Niebuhr reflected that the drummer was a type of modern man who had been liberated from discipline and sacrifice, but "without achieving any new loyalty that might qualify the brutal factors of human life." "It is better that life incarnate some ideal value," he mused, "even if mixed with illusion, than that it should express nothing but the will to live." Certainly some warriors may be under the illusion that American power is always exercised with virtue and always for a just cause, but critics should not overlook the ideals of altruism, teamwork, *esprit de corps* and sacrifice that this community sustains. The military is neither the highest nor lowest of human centers of loyalty. It is a relative good and a constitutive element of the state as an order of creation.

Sixteen

The Warrior and the Pacifist

There dwell and toil, in the British village of Dumdrudge, usually some 500 souls. From these. . . there are successively selected, during the French War, say 30 able-bodied men: Dumdrudge, at her own expense, has suckled and nursed them; she has, not without difficulty and sorrow, fed them up to manhood, and even trained them to crafts, so that one can weave, another build, another hammer, and the weakest can stand under thirty stone avoirdupois. Nevertheless, amid much weeping and swearing, they are selected; all dressed in red; and shipped away, at the public charges, some two thousand miles, or say only to the south of Spain; and fed there till wanted. And now to that same spot in the south of Spain, are 30 similar French artisans, from a French Dumdrudge, in like manner wending: Till at length, after infinite effort, the two parties come into actual juxtaposition; and Thirty stands fronting Thirty, each with a gun in his hand. Straightway the word 'Fire!' is given: and they blow the souls out of one another; and in the place of sixty brisk useful craftsmen, the world has sixty dead carcasses, which it must bury, and anew shed tears for. Had these men any quarrel!? Busy as the Devil is, not the smallest! . . . Their Governors had fallen out: and, instead of shooting one another, had the cunning to make these poor blockheads shoot--Alas, so it is in Deutschland, and hitherto in all other lands.

Carlyle, *Sartor Resartus*

Perpetual peace is a futile dream, dominated by internationally minded pacifists--the jellyfish of the world--who are constantly working to change Armistice day into disarmament day.

George S. Patton, Jr., 1932

The soldier accepts the option of pacifism as the hallmark of a democratic society and recognizes the duty to defend the conscientious objector. The soldier even admires the *classical* or *vocational* pacifist for his attempt to incarnate an absolute ideal and who, like himself is willing to suffer if not die for his belief. The vocational pacifist understands that he has been "called" to witness against a culture of violence. Whether that witness springs from religious or secular roots, any form of calculus as to prudence or the utilitarian greater good is unimportant. He is willing to be a "fool for the sake of Christ," or any other ultimate concern, religious or secular. The vocational pacifist knows that he will always be a member of a lonely minority, much like the religious of Catholic communities who possess the gifts to practice the virtues of celibacy, obedience, and poverty. He does not universalize his calling, knowing that peacemaking can take a variety of forms. In personally turning the other cheek to violence, the classical pacifist admits that it may not be either possible or prudent for the majority of citizens to do so.

For his part, the soldier knows his vocation involves moral ambiguity regarding coercion but, in eschewing ethical legalism, he believes violence is sometimes necessary to protect the defenseless. The warrior believes that had the Good Samaritan been on the road to Jericho a few minutes earlier, he would not have piously folded his hands while the thieves assaulted their victim. Like Kant, he knows that the only true good is a pure will or character. The warrior shares the moral world of ambiguity with the police, his civilian counterpart. He appreciates that the classical pacifist is neither elitist nor condemnatory of his vocation. The classical pacifist acknowledges there are religiously deep and sensitive soldiers whose altruism and sacrificial motives are as deep as his. Both agree that their forms of peacemaking are complementary rather than antithetical.

Even Patton, in spite of his protestations of "loving war," knew the warrior's vocation was fraught with moral ambiguity. Of the hundreds of poems he composed during the Second World War, his favorite was "The Soul Speaks:"

> Here is Honor, the dying knight
> And here is Truth, the snuffed out light
> And here is Faith, the broken staff
> And there is Knowledge, the throttled laugh,
> And here is Fame, the lost surprise,
> Virtue, the uncontested prize,
> And Sacrifice, the suicide
> And there, the wilted flower, Pride,
> Under the crust of things that die
> Living, unfathomed, here am I.

While even the most ardent warrior can respect the sincerity of the vocational pacifist, he has little patience for the *prudential* or *pragmatic* pacifist who uses pacifism as a tool of statecraft. Pacifists who believe that the "cross of Christ is triumphant in time," or that "turning the other cheek" actually "works" in the rough-n-tumble of foreign affairs, he believes, have a deficient anthropology and are blind to the lessons of history. Original sin and the will to power of racial, ethnic, and national collectives are frightful. To imagine that unilateral disarmament would have tamed the inhumane ideologies of the Neros, Hitlers, and Stalins of this world is utopian if not delusional. Visions of the lion and the lamb bedding down together belong beyond, not within, history.

During the 1960s I heard a gentle lady tell Reinhold Niebuhr that the USSR would become more pacific if Christians would pray for the conversion of Stalin. "We have been building arms," she remonstrated, "when we should have been on our knees. The power of prayer is infinite," she continued. "Who knows. It might soften the heart of Stalin."

While Niebuhr treated her gently, he was pitiless in destroying the sentimental illusions she conveyed. President Woodrow Wilson's hope "that national morality can be made to act like individual morality" is a chimera based on fantasy rather than empirical realism. Love becomes sentimental if it tries to replace justice. Niebuhr's principle--"Love can only go *beyond* justice, it can never take the *place* of justice"--has been a moral canon I have always remembered. In selective cases an application of *intra-national* non-violence may achieve some limited goals. The achievements of Martin Luther King and Gandhi have proved that "soul force" and vicarious suffering can be effective in certain selected and limited situations. The warrior would remind the pragmatic pacifist, however, that the British soldiers who refused to drive their trains and tanks over prostrate Indians came from a Western culture that respects human life.

Martin Luther King's pacific and powerful civil rights movement succeeded because its protest was within the context of American civil liberties and a culture that had Judaic-Christian rootage. This double legacy, at least in principle, respected persons whatever the color of their skin. Without this indigenous moral soil, the Bull Connors, George Wallaces, and the KKK may not have yielded. No one should think, however, that prudential pacifism should be a nation's strategy for *extra-national* conflict. Nation-states are the most predatory and predacious of all human collectives. While vicarious sacrifice is sometimes practiced by heroic individuals, I know of no historic instance where a nation-state has voluntarily endured crucifixion. The litany is long and mournful regarding the massacre of minorities--Muslims in Kashmir, Hindus in Pakistan, Jews in Hitler's Germany and Tsarist Russia, Bahaists in Iran, Kurds and Armenians in Turkey, Koreans in Japan, Christians in Sudan and Nigeria, Serbs in Austro-Hungary. The present carnage in the former Yugoslavia started five centuries ago and has every promise of continuing for another five. At present, portions of Africa are tribal bloodbaths. Tribal conflict, tragically, appears likely to continue on every continent until the end of time.

Universal visions of our common spirituality and brotherhood are impotent in contrast to the visible and particularistic loyalties close at hand. Tens of thousands die every year for their families, tribes, and nations. But who willingly dies for the United Nations or the World Federalists?

Pragmatic pacifists cannot produce any historical example where the weakness and unilateral disarmament of a nation reduced the imperialism and will to power of its enemy. There is no evidence that the ruthless, fanatical allegiance to blood, tribe and race that has unleashed such rivers of blood in the 20th century is likely to diminish--no sign of its abating. Sentimentality is thus the ever-present camp-follower of the pacifist. As an undergraduate I once asked one of my pacifist Hamline professors, "What would you do if you saw a German soldier trying to violate your sister?" He replied with pious virtue, "I would try to get *between* them." I neglected to ask the follow-up question, "Would your sister have agreed with your 'heroic' stance?" During the decades after the Second World War, China and the USSR repeatedly co-opted Western pacifists with their periodic "peace campaigns." Ignoring the Sino-Soviet propaganda about Western warmongering, George Orwell was one of the few intellectuals who had 20-20 vision during that era. "No ordinary man could be such a fool as to believe," he mused, "that nice words canceled hostile acts or that dictatorship could be a sort of democracy." The Peace Campaign of the 1950s reached its climax with the famous Stockholm Peace Appeal, for which Picasso designed a special dove. It was signed by millions of people, including the whole North Korean Army just before its attack on the South.

A major error of the pragmatic pacifist is to believe that violence is the inevitable expression of ill will, and non-violence of good will; that violence is therefore intrinsically evil and non-violence intrinsically good. If we admit, however, that coercion is sometimes ethically justifiable albeit morally problematical, we cannot draw an absolute line between violent and non-violent coercion. Kant and Niebuhr agree--"only good will is *intrinsically* good." Speaking of good will, I have noticed that, although campus pacifists may eschew physical killing, a few are quite accomplished as psychological killers. Caustic and hateful remarks can destroy at least as effectively--and as painfully--as the sword. Such pacifists have forgotten the wisdom of the *Talmud*: "The power of life and death reside in the tongue."

Gandhi's boycott of British cotton during the Great Depression resulted in the malnourishment of children in England, just as the Allied blockade of Germany in World War I caused the death of German civilians and children, who were reduced to eating dogs and cats (the latter known as "roof rabbits") and to concocting bread from a mixture of potato peelings and sawdust. The Allied passive and *non-violent* blockade from 1914-1918 resulted in 752,106 deaths, almost equal to the 800,000 German civilians killed by our *violent* bombing during the Second World War.

There is no absolute distinction between non-violent and violent types of coercion. If a period of violence can overthrow an unjust system and clear the way for a relatively more just political order, there is no ethical basis for ruling out either war or revolution.

Pacifists claim to be persons of sensitive spirit. I suspect it is the horror of war, as expressed by Siegfried Sasoon in "Aftermath, March 1919" that shapes their view on violence:

> Have you forgotten yet?
> Look down, and swear by the slain of the War that
>   you'll never forget.
> Do you remember the dark months you held the
>   sector at Mametz,
> The nights you watched and wired and dug and
>   piled sandbags on parapets?
> Do you remember the rats; and the stench
> Of corpses rotting in front of the front-line trench
> And dawn coming, dirty-white, and chill with a
>   hopeless rain?
> Do you ever stop and ask, "Is it all going to happen again?"
> Do you remember that hour of din before the
>   attack --
> And the anger, the blind compassion that seized
>   and shook you then
> As you peered at the doomed and haggard faces of
>   your men?
> Do you remember the stretcher-cases lurching
>   back
> With dying eyes and lolling heads--those ashen-grey

> Masks of the lads who once were keen and kind and gay?
> Have you forgotten yet? . . .
> Look up, and swear by the green of the spring that you'll never forget.

If violence is to be justified, as St. Augustine stated, it should be as a last resort and its terror must have the tempo of a surgeon's skill. Healing, too, must follow quickly upon its wounds. To the end of history, the peace of the world will be gained by strife. It can never be a perfect peace, but it can always be more perfect than it is. The purpose of violence, therefore, is not a final end to conflict but a more just peace than presently exists. The perennial tragedy of *Homo sapiens* is that pacifists who attempt to cultivate the spiritual elements of our character usually do so by misunderstanding or divorcing themselves from the problems of collective humankind. The brutal nature of our collectives are there for all who have eyes to see.

Seventeen

The Case For Universal Military Service

> We have tried since the birth of our nation to promote our love of peace by a display of weakness. This course has failed us utterly.
>
> General George C. Marshall, 1945

Shortly before his death in 1968, Bobby Kennedy was one of the most popular speakers on American college campuses. Students respected his honesty, responded to his charisma, and trusted him to tell the truth as he agonized with them over the ethics of the military draft.

"How many of you favor an all-volunteer military service?" he would shout. A sea of uplifted hands would be the response.

"And how many of you would be willing to serve?" he would continue. Scarcely a hand would be raised.

"Now, don't you see," he would yell, "that's the problem!"

Despite the popularly held view of the sufficiency of our professional military, I contend, like Kennedy, that a vibrant democracy should have a citizen-soldier military. The following points are crucial to the issue.

1. **In A Democracy Equal Rights Imply Equal Obligations.** A professional, all-volunteer force contradicts a fundamental principle upon which our nation was founded: that benefits and burdens should be distributed as equitably as possible. During the Civil War an affluent WASP northerner could pay $90 to have an immigrant Irishman take his place for him in the draft. During the Vietnam war university student exemptions and high grade-point averages allowed economic and intellectual elites to continue life as usual while their blue-collar brothers fought and died in Asian jungles. Psychologists believe that much campus hell-raising during the 60s arose from students' repressed anger and self-hate resulting from their knowing that they were unfairly privileged.

Racial demographics make clear the mercenary nature of the "volunteer" military. Thirty-five per cent of the army and 22 per cent of the Marine Corps is black. If present trends continue, we may soon have a military whose members are primarily drawn from various minority groups, a black and brown army defending a mainly white nation.

Military service in a democracy is a citizen's obligation not because it may demand the giving up of one's life, but because arms protect the state that is responsible for the giving and protecting of human rights. Such rights are not automatic, like the sunrise, gravity, and winter snow. If duty is not connected to liberty, rights are taken for granted. Jefferson once wrote, "There is a debt of service due from every man to his country, proportioned to the bounties which nature and fortune have measured to him." Whatever his social estate, no American can ever repay the indebtedness he owes prior generations for the gift of freedom. A year or two in the service is valuable and visible down payment on that debt.

In the 1960s several of my students who were pacifists asked me to accompany them to their draft boards and vouch for their integrity. I was pleased to be asked, for while I did not agree with their position, I believed they were sincere. I was deeply impressed by the integrity of the members of draft boards. They bridged all age levels and there seemed to be a sincere attempt to discern the motivation, integrity, and consistency of the student petitioners. Prior to the war in Vietnam, one achieved non-combatant status only by meeting a narrow theistic criterion--one had to claim God demanded turning the other cheek to all violence. Now humanists and secularists who claimed a pacifist philosophy of life were granted exemption from military service. Every student that I supported was granted a form of alternative service. (A lad named Kevin, unfortunately, assumed the system was entirely corrupt. He went to Canada and I subsequently lost contact with him.)

Many liberals have 20/20 vision in seeing the injustice of reducing social programs for the poor. Some of those same liberals, however, are ethically myopic in *not* seeing the injustice of the mercenary nature of our military--of using the marginalized members of our society to enable the bourgeoisie and their children to pursue privatist concerns.

Three decades after his service in Vietnam, Colin L. Powell, in *My American Journey*, was still angry with the political leaders who supplied the manpower for that war:

> The policies--determining who would be drafted and who would be deferred, who would serve and who would escape, who would die and who would live--were an antidemocratic disgrace. I

can never forgive a leadership that said, in effect: These young men--poorer, less educated, less privileged--are expendable "economic cannon fodder"--but the rest are too good to risk. This raw discrimination strikes me as the most damaging to the ideal that all Americans are created equal and owe equal allegiance to their country.

   2. **Universal Service Militates Against Caste, Both Military and Social.** Military service is a partial solvent to caste, whether geographic, racial, social or educational. While the military is, of necessity, based on a chain of command, the draft forces comradeship among those who would not normally associate with one another--who, indeed, might otherwise not even be aware of each other's existence. Black, brown, white, and yellow are compelled to form platoons and companies. Ivy League graduates have to associate with those who went to Mediocre U., rural "rubes" with "city slickers," privileged suburbanites with street-smart kids from the inner city. Military service in Israel, for example, has aided the forces of homogenization in nation-building by bringing Ashkenazic and Sephardic Jews together. The former, of European culture and long dominant in Israeli society, must learn to fight and work with their social "inferiors," the Middle Eastern Jews.

   At a time when school busing is waning and the formation of social castes is both increasing and hardening, universal service would assure us that members of each generation would have at least one experience that lifts them out of their region, background, and class.

   When a state chooses to pay either its less fortunate citizens or mercenaries for undertaking military responsibilities it no longer wishes to assume, there can be severe consequences. Seventy years before the death of Julius Caesar, the army of Rome became professional when Caius Marius offered pay for service in his campaign against the African king Jugurtha. Before Marius, bearing arms was a citizen's duty; afterwards, soldiers owed their allegiance to their generals rather than Rome. The generals' rivalry hastened Rome's decline. While such a situation is hardly conceivable in our country, a professional army may tend toward hard-line political opinions far more than one that is representative of the at-large population. If the United States loses respect for the military, it is reasonable to suppose that the military will lose respect for America. Then Prussianism, a coup d'etat, or a "Seven Days in May" scenario might become possible, despite our traditions of military deference to political authority.

3. The Draft Contributes To The Shaping Of Character. It has been about 35 years since President Kennedy set forth the challenge--"Ask not what your country can do for you; ask rather what you can do for your country." Until Vietnam, few questioned the nation's right to demand a year or two of one's life as the price of citizenship. Now we may be losing our sense of participation in the great American Experiment. We seem increasingly surfeited with narcissism, privatism, materialism, and hedonism.

Michael Blumenthal, a Vietnam draft dodger and the author of *Sympathetic Magic*, deliberately inhaled canvas dust to revive a childhood history of asthma. Now he realizes he missed something by evading military duty. "To put it bluntly, those who served have something I don't have: realism, discipline, masculinity (kind of a dirty word these days), resilience, tenacity, resourcefulness." Draft dodgers may have turned out to be "better dancers, choreographers and painters," he adds, but "I am not at all sure that those who fought the war didn't turn out to be better men, in the best sense of the word."

Obviously, there are experiences other than the military that instill "realism, discipline, and masculinity." Not everyone who didn't serve in Vietnam (or any other war) failed to acquire these laudable characteristics. Then too, there is no guarantee military service will make one a "better man," as attested to by the many Vietnam veterans who became hollow shells as a result of their experience.

During Vietnam many members of the academy excused student behavior in avoiding the draft. They stood mute as men wore girls' panties to their physicals, faked asthma attacks, put sugar in their urine samples, starved or gorged themselves to avoid weight limits, got women pregnant or joined the National Guard in droves to avoid combat. For too many it was a case of the end justifying the means.

American youth who are anxious about adolescence, acne, sexuality, political correctness, "cool" clothes, the latest computer software, a fine compact disk collection, and eventually finding a home in a good corporation are a sad lot when it comes to certain Israeli sabras, Kurds, Arabs, Croatians, Serbs, Haitians, Azerbaijanis, and others who are simply worried about their countries and their lives.

I do not mean to mythologize or romanticize either war or the military, but there is something to be said for the dose of realism that comes with military service. So much of existence is banal, passionless and non-communal. Maybe life is not meant to be lived just for having "fun" and being obsessed with our own skin. Maybe we mature by going through the dark tunnel of danger and mortality in camaraderie and shared purpose and sacrifice. Perhaps there *is* something missing in a generation of hypersensitive, "untainted" men; something real and deeper than can be dismissed with the facile indictment of "macho."

There is little doubt that certain of the warrior virtues--discipline, neatness, duty, and *esprit de corps*--are prized in American corporations as they seek retired military officers. Like a Notre Dame football coach, George Patton gave his officers in tank school a rousing affirmation of the necessity of discipline:

> Discipline is not a foolish thing, it is not a demeaning thing, it is a vital thing. Lack of discipline at play means the loss of a few yards. Lack of discipline in war means death or defeat. The prize for a game is nothing. The prize for this war is the greatest of all prizes--freedom. It is by discipline alone that all your efforts, all your patriotism, shall not have been in vain. Without it heroism is futile. You will die for nothing. With DISCIPLINE you are IRRESISTIBLE.

Liberal societies are rightly repelled by military regimentation. Yet there is another side as well, as summed up by Woodrow Wilson:

> A friend of mine made a very poignant remark to me one day. He said, "Did you ever see a family that hung its son's yardstick or a ledger or a spade up over the mantelpiece?" But how many of you have seen the lad's rifle, his musket, hung up! Well, why? A musket is a barbarous thing. The spade and yardstick and ledger are the symbols of peace and steady business; why not hang them up? Because they do not represent self-sacrifice. They do not glorify you in the same sense that the musket does, because when you took that musket at the call of your country you risked everything

and knew you could not get anything. The most that you could do was to come back alive, but after you came back alive, there was a halo about you.

4. Universal Service Is An Appropriate Response To Worldly Reality. With the collapse of the Soviet Union, the United States is the only remaining super-power in the world. Even now, if history teaches any lesson worth remembering, the demonic virus that possessed a Hitler, Mussolini, Stalin, and a Tojo may be mutating in some adolescent and brutish breast. While our geographical strata record the biological ascent of man, there is little evidence of *Homo sapiens'* moral evolution. The pages of history will likely continue to be bloody, as I've stated already, until the end of time.

In World War I, legions of American doughboys were thrown into the trenches with virtually no preparation for combat. Upon noticing 100 men of the Rainbow division huddled around a sergeant, Douglas MacArthur was about to reprimand them when the sergeant explained, "Sir, I am teaching them how to load rifles!" At the beginning of World War II, the American military stood in 16th place among the world's armies, with only 132,069 Americans in uniform--fewer than the Portuguese or the Greeks. After Pearl Harbor we were forced to commit large numbers of poorly and hastily trained soldiers to combat. (Obsolete and ineffective equipment made matters worse: During MacArthur's heroic Battle of Bataan, 70 percent of the mortar shells proved to be duds and four out of five hand grenades failed to explode. Our soldiers fought with World War I left-overs, like the obsolete Enfield rifles and the shiny pith helmets.) The eggs began to hatch from our ostrich-like, head-in-the-sand position we had assumed during the inter-war period.

The lives of thousands of our soldiers could have been saved by a peacetime draft. In *Crusade In Europe*, Eisenhower makes this prudential observation:

> Until world order is an accomplished fact and universal disarmament a logical result, it will always be a crime to excuse men from the types and kinds of training that will give them a decent chance for survival in battle. Many of the crosses standing in Tunisia today are witness to this truth.

5. Military Service and the American Presidency.

For many veterans it is troublesome that President Bill Clinton did not serve in the military. Within the first month of his presidency, he unilaterally attempted to compel the armed services to accept out-of-the-closet homosexuals. To warriors, it signaled his "in your face" contempt toward the intimate bond of their profession. At worst, the action revealed his unresolved animus toward the military; at best, it displayed an ignorance of military culture.

A president with an existential experience of the military, whatever his view on homosexuality, would have moved with greater prudence. Dialogue with General Colin Powell and the other joint chiefs should have taken place. Fortunately, the House and Senate Armed Services Committees aborted Clinton's initiative and forced a compromise. This much, however, is sure. There are still too many White House staff who betray an anti-military animus engendered by their feelings about Vietnam when they were undergraduates.

In *My American Journey*, General Powell reported the following:

One day, my assistant, Lieutenant General Barry McCaffrey, went to the White House. (He) passed a young staffer and said, "Hello, there," to which she replied with upturned nose, "We don't talk to soldiers around here." McCaffrey was the winner of three Silver Stars and still bore disfiguring arm wounds suffered in Vietnam. He commanded one of the crack divisions in Desert Storm. The young woman's comment rocketed back to the Pentagon and whipped through the place like a free electron.

A review of many military and veteran's magazines reveals a high level of distrust of, if not disdain for, President Clinton. They label his attempt to include homosexuals in the military as "political pandering."

The Clinton military-gay fiasco does, however, raise the question: "Is presidential leadership enhanced by service in the armed forces?" Over the years, Americans have put six experienced generals into the presidency--George Washington, Andrew Jackson, William Henry Harrison, Zachary Taylor, Ulysses S. Grant, and Dwight Eisenhower. We tend to turn to generals when we are fed up with existing political processes. They give us a sense of safety and security in difficult times. Sixteen of our presidents fought in battle, the ultimate physical test: Washington, Monroe, Jackson, William Henry Harrison, Taylor, Pierce, Grant, Hayes, Garfield, Benjamin Harrison, McKinley, Theodore Roosevelt, Truman, Eisenhower, Kennedy, and Bush. Eisenhower helped us negotiate the socio-political backwash of World War II and extricated us from Korea. He had superb political instincts and special personal qualities. Eisenhower was a moderate with "no hard edges," the Democrats were tired, and we wanted a comfortable change. It was the same story with Ulysses S. Grant. Congress was in turmoil and Andrew Johnson, having barely survived impeachment, was wildly unpopular. Northerners worried about what southern whites were doing to blacks. Grant was the little quiet general, the hero of Vicksburg and Appomattox, who would put things right.

Great generals don't always make great presidents, of course. Grant saved the union, but as president he surrounded himself with corrupt officials and advisers. Harrison didn't live long enough to make his mark; having caught pneumonia in a cold rain during his inaugural, he died a month later. General Taylor, arguably the most uneducated man ever to win the White House, died after only 16 months in office, also without leaving much of an impression.

Nor are all great presidents and statesmen necessarily ex-military men. Our greatest president, Abraham Lincoln, possessed a genius of character and leadership that military service may not have augmented. Even so, a sojourn in the army might have given him some insight in how to deal more effectively with a succession of Union generals who were reluctant to engage the enemy. In any case, on the whole I believe that the leadership qualities and skills derived from military experience can be beneficial in the office of president.

Military rank at any level probably enlarges rather than diminishes the quality of leadership. Presidents Theodore Roosevelt, Truman, Kennedy, Carter, Reagan, Bush and others were not impaired for having served. For most it was a time of testing. The experience deepened their worldly discernment, and their patriotism, and it honed their leadership and executive abilities. Those who are suspicious of the military will, of course, point out possible dangers. A military "lifer," upon elevation to the presidency, might too easily entertain the military option in problematic international confrontations.

To date, that has not happened. Eisenhower did not wear a hawkish mantle, nor, given retired General

Powell's reluctance regarding Desert Storm, does it seem that this would become his stance should he become president. During the past half-century, military bravado has more often come from the civilians of the State Department than from the Joint Chiefs of Staff. The latter know the bitter lessons of Vietnam, Lebanon, Somalia, and elsewhere--that issues of political instability are rarely solved by military intervention.

It seems certain that President Clinton will never have the complete respect of the warrior. Many in the military are conflicted by a love-hate relationship to their Commander-in-Chief. Military code demands that soldiers honor their superiors. But Clinton bears the tragic legacy of avoiding the draft and a barely concealed contempt for the military profession, and he seemingly refuses to learn the simple skill of returning a proper salute. His required presence at ceremonies on the 50th anniversary of the D-Day landings, and at Arlington National Cemetery, the Korean War Memorial, and especially at the Vietnam Memorial must be a terrible psychic burden for him.

In looking toward the future, it would be prudent to be wary of a pacifistic, "let's talk this out," chief executive who believes moral suasion is the universal solution for international discord. We need to fear two extremes: 1. An inability to use force when it is prudent to do so; 2. A military rush-to-judgment rooted in a need either to prove presidential manhood or to divert attention away from internal national dilemmas. Military professionals are increasingly worried that our armed forces are being used in Africa, the Caribbean, the Mediterranean and elsewhere on tasks for which they are ill-trained. That is, as an external police force with quasi-social worker, "nation-building," agendas.

A prudent president will recognize the peace-keeping attempts of United Nations blue-helmet operations for what they are: exercises in wishful thinking.

The fact is, if there is peace, peacekeepers are unnecessary; if there is war, peacekeepers are unavailing. The U.N. blue-helmets can neither insure collective security nor halt aggression. They are little more than hand-holding and temporizing operations by means of which the Great Powers pretend to do something. We have seen the catastrophic failure of such operations in Somalia and Bosnia. In Somalia, units from several countries called their capitals to ask whether or not to follow the orders of the local U.N. commander! This was not an army, it was group therapy in fatigues.

Colin Powell is right when he says, "The will to build a nation originates from within its people, not from the outside." It is utopian to think we can substitute our version of democracy for hundreds of years of tribalism. "In the end," said Henry Kissinger, "peace can be achieved only by hegemony or by balance of power. There is no other way."

Our president is designated by the Constitution as our armed forces' Commander-in-Chief whether or not he wishes that power and irrespective of his attitude toward the warrior. It seems obvious, therefore, that even a brief experience in the military would enhance the sophistication of his use of that awesome power. All presidents, by word, gesture, and the disposition of their soul, should honor those who have pledged their lives as the guarantee of our respective freedoms.

6. **The Military and Worldly Reality:** Our power, including military force, must be appropriate to our worldly commitments. Without a military force of appropriate size and quality, a future conflict might force us into the nuclear option. We badly need a Reinhold Niebuhr today to refresh our anthropological realism, to bring the Children of Light and the Children of Darkness into dialogue. If the latter need visions of hope, modest though they may be, certainly the former could use a dose

of global realism. Our intellectual fare needs to be the 13th chapter of Romans as well as the Beatitudes; St. Augustine as well as St. Francis; Hobbes, Machiavelli, and Lenin along with the contemporary Jane Fondas, Martin Luther Kings, and the flower children.

When campus radicals cry, "All war is wrong; it's better to talk things out," I wonder who taught them the history of the 1930s and 40s. Singing for peace and cheering speakers who denounce the Pentagon, oil companies, multinational corporations, and soldiers as "baby killers" may be therapeutic as a catharsis. But while the Children of Light strum guitars, the Children of Darkness are busy taking target practice.

The world, as Martin Luther reminded us, cannot be ruled by a crucifix. Violence is endemic to the human condition and is globally on the increase. Only Australia, of all the continents, has been exempt from serious national and international conflict in recent times. We must overcome our love/hate relationship with the military--embracing it in times of war, despising it in times of peace. Whatever conspiracy theories we may have about the Pentagon and the Joint Chiefs of Staff, and however demonic we may believe the military to be, it will not, somehow, go away. What is at issue is *not the fact* of having a military *but what kind* of military is appropriate to a democratic society.

In 1925 Albert Einstein and Mahatma Gandhi signed an Anti-Conscription Manifesto that stated in part:

> It is debasing human dignity to force men to give up their life, or to inflict death against their will, or without conviction as to the justice of their action. The State which thinks itself entitled to force its citizens to go to war will never pay proper regard to the value and happiness of their lives in peace. Moreover, by conscription the

militarist spirit of aggressiveness is implanted in the whole male population at the most impressionable age. By training for war men come to consider war unavoidable and even as desirable.

The genius of Einstein as a physicist stands in sharp contrast to his naive comprehension of statecraft. At the time, his cheap platitudes cost him nothing. But within the decade they began to have a tragic harvest that led to the Holocaust and the death of 6,000,000 of his fellow Jews. Whatever their example and however "spiritual" their views, pacifists too, have blood on their hands. This much is sure, a nation that undermines its military institutions and denigrates the military virtues of its soldiers cannot long defend itself against totalitarian regimes that do not share its commitment to liberal principles.

Eighteen

Do Intellectuals Have Blood On Their Hands?

During his service in the Russian army, Leo Tolstoy saw one of his brother officers strike a man who had fallen out of ranks. Tolstoy remonstrated:

"Are you not ashamed to treat a fellow human being in this way? Have you not read the Gospels?"

The other officer replied: "And have you not read Army Orders?"

One of the pastimes that I have enjoyed with a coterie of faculty friends is to debate which, of all the books that have been written, is your particular *summun bonum*? "If you had the power to require *all* college students to read but *one book*," is my query, "What might it be?" Obviously, a religion professor might select the Bible, St. Augustine's *Confessions*, or John Bunyan's *Pilgrim's Progress*. A philosophy professor, however, might choose Plato's *Republic*; a political scientist, Machiavelli's *The Prince* or *The Federalist Papers*; a biologist, Darwin's *Origin of Species*; an English professor, an anthology of Shakespeare or John Milton. And so it goes. Most of us would dip into our memory bank of Great Books for our selection. Our discussions never arrive at a consensus because we are each captive to our own discipline.

My selection was Dostoevski's *The Brothers Karamazov*. Although set in the 19th century, this classic illuminates the universal enigmas that confront every generation. The themes of freedom and determinism, immortality, conscience, duty, unbelief, justice, and more are dealt with in memorable fashion through the development of unforgettable characters. In their personal struggles, the members of the Karamazov family are a microcosm of the family of man.

A professor of modern European history, however, always made a case for *The Treason of the Intellectuals (La Trahison des Clercs)*, 1928, by an obscure author, Julian Benda. Benda was a French journalist who explored the etiology of the Great War. The traditional explanations--secret alliances, disparities in population growth between Germany and France, ethnic hostility, political personalities, and the shopworn Freudian or Marxist interpretations--Benda viewed as of minor importance.

Why, Benda asked, was not the early 20th century the harbinger of a golden age? After all, the general spirit of the period was liberal and enlightened. Man was out of the woods and had sloughed off the bestial residue of evolution. Age-old superstitions, prejudices, and hatreds had been laid to rest. Poverty, ignorance, and dogmas (ecclesiastical or otherwise) were on the run. Was not man on an automatic escalator of scientific and moral progress?

Apparently not, for if he were, why did an entire generation, the flower of German, French, English and Russian manhood, perish between 1914 and 1918? What, Benda wondered, had gone wrong? Why had an ugly ten-mile-wide scar from the English Channel to Switzerland become the graveyard of 10 million men and aborted all hope for a golden age? How could a bomb thrown into the carriage of a minor prince in an obscure little province of the Austrian-Hungarian empire bring about a holocaust?

Simply put, Benda made the case that the hands of European intellectuals were stained with the blood of World War I because they ceased *being* intellectuals in the classic sense.

He was quite right, I believe. Until recent times intellectuals were stateless persons because they were loyal to transcendental values. Great thinkers such as Plato, Aristotle, Augustine and Thomas Aquinas studied the nature of universals such as beauty, honor, truth, justice, prudence, courage and the like. Such transcendental virtues were the eternal norms that governed the vagaries of personal and institutional life "below." Like their spiritual counterparts, the clergy, intellectuals had a vertical vision connected to the *real* (i.e., transcendental) world. Their "real" or "true" world is not the sensory world of our existence. Their purpose was to understand, enlarge and transmit the nature of this eternal world to those caught up in the mire and muck of everyday existence.

The purpose of the ivory tower, like that of the cloister, was to provide a necessary detachment from everything partial and provincial. Intellectuals, by definition, are supposed to be apolitical, passionless, and detached from factional, particular, and national loyalties. If intellectuals mucked about in the profane, from whom would the common man learn the nature and gain the vision of the Truth and of God? From the time of the Stoics, many intellectuals believed that all human beings, whatever their race, gender, or creed, were part of a divine *nous* (a divine spark or consciousness) which was their contact with the Divine Mind. The particularities of nationality, class, and race were superficial characteristics and not the true essence of what it meant to be a member of *Homo sapiens*.

The vision of an intellectual, therefore, is that of the eagle and not that of the worm. He sees reality, history and humankind holistically, not in segments. His intellectual force is centripetal, uniting men on the basis of their shared, catholic, and immutable nature. The credo of the intellectual is a secularized version of St. Paul's proclamation: "In Christ Jesus, there is neither Greek nor Roman, slave nor free, male nor female, you are all *one*." While constantly frustrated by the hubris of rival princes, the vision of the medieval Church was always that of a *corpus Christianum*, a universal Christian and humane community. Christ's death and resurrection had established His Church and a reign of God that leveled all particularities. For 1500 years this intellectual vision was fairly successful in suppressing many of the animosities of tribe and clan.

Although the seeds of the academic intellectuals betrayal of their profession began in the 16th century with the Reformation and the rise of nationalism, the full effects of their apostasy took place in the 19th and 20th centuries. The intellectuals of Germany, England, France, and Italy participated in "the nationalization of the mind." Xenophobia replaced the spiritual unity of *Homo sapiens*. Jingoism exalted particular cultures at the expense of a common human culture. Hatred "of man from the *outside*" increased as did rejection of and scorn for everything that was not from "his own home (nation)." Intellectuals were transformed into "the spiritual militia of the material." To use a medical metaphor, they became national physicians injecting the bourgeoisie with hyper-active ideological nostrums. Scholars became whores. Their words were aimed not at the minds of men but at their passions.

Benda maintained that what Darwin had limited to the biological realm, these intellectuals applied to human and social reality. Social Darwinians proclaimed war was a "biological necessity," a carrying out among mankind of "the natural law." Nations must progress or decay--"there is no standing still." Bernhardi of Germany said his country must choose "world power or downfall." Among all nations, he averred, Germany "is in social-political respects at the head of all progress in culture" but is "compressed into narrow, unnatural limits." She cannot attain her "great moral ends" without increased political power, an enlarged sphere of influence and new territory.

Having become culturally myopic, European intellectuals refused to see beyond their own borders. Each asked his countrymen to remain faithful to their native genius--including "French *cooking*, French *art*, French *fashions*, even French *hair-dressing*." "Science must not soar beyond the frontiers," stated the German philosopher Guisebrecht, "but must be national, be German." In the past, intellectuals taught that the State should be just. Now they asked only that it be strong. Unlike St. Augustine who saw a *Justem Bellum*, a "just war," as a tragic necessity, war now became gloried for its own sake. Nietzsche, for example, sanctified military life and the war instinct apart from any political aim:

> The values of the warrior aristocracy are founded on a powerful bodily constitution, excellent health, without forgetting all that is necessary to the upkeep of that overflowing vigor--war, adventure, hunting, dancing, physical games and exercises, and in general everything which implies a robust, free and joyous activity. That audacity of noble races, a mad, absurd, spontaneous audacity, is their indifference and scorn for all safety of body, for life, and comfort . . . The superb blond beast wandering in search of prey and carnage . . . The terrible gaiety and profound joy felt by

heroes in all destruction, in all the pleasures of victory and cruelty.

Each nation saw itself as the sole judge of its actions. Moral universals were deemed to be "metaphysical fog." Having lost hold of religion, politics became the passion of intellectuals. The hatred of Satan and sin that previously had been universal and personal was transferred to classes and nationalities. When conflict threatened, modern scholars seized ideological swords instead of the classical weapons of prayers and supplications. In place of God, a mystic "national soul" became identified as the divine host in plebeian minds. Romantic nationalism--Goddess France, Nordic Germany, Mother Russia, etc.--became the altar of devotion. When European governments in 1914 pushed the mobilization button, some academics joined the riffraff in the streets, waving their handkerchiefs and shouting, "Mobilization!" Like much of the rabble, they were quickly converted from Marx to Mars.

After the German devastation of neutral Belgium in August, 1914, 93 German professors issued a Manifesto addressed "To the Civilized World" proclaiming the civilizing effects of German culture. "It is not true that we have criminally violated the neutrality of Belgium," pontificated the intellectuals. "It is not true that our troops have brutally destroyed Louvain." However imposing the signatories' names and reputations--Harnack, Sudermann, Humperdinck, Roentgen, Hauptmann--the ashes of the great medieval Louvain library were a mute witness to their hypocrisy.

It is my conviction that many American intellectuals are repeating the folly of their colleagues of three generations ago. They have forgotten the warning of John Wycliffe to the clergy of his era--"If golde ruste, what will iron do?" Since isolation is often the lot of intellectuals, too many seek to relieve their sense of impotence and of not being taken seriously through intense political activism. In the search for recognition, status, and notoriety, they have exchanged the lectern for the bully pulpit. They exacerbate their students' passions rather than inform their minds. For some, the political loyalties of their students count for more than the quality of their minds and souls. Others lose the individuality of their students by weighing too heavily the external factors and superficial particularities of skin, gender, class, sexual preference, and ethnicity.

Most universities of the Third World have forfeited any claim to being centers of serious intellectual endeavor because they have become politicized. Tragically, this is increasingly true of many distinguished American colleges, especially in the humanities and social sciences.

Many academics believe they are renaissance persons, but too many have a habit of generalizing from a narrow field of expertise to claimed wisdom as wide as the waterfront. They are guilty of the "As a" syndrome: "*As a* philosopher, I think the budget of the Pentagon *should be cut.*" "*As a* sociologist, I have concluded that America *does not need* the B-l bomber." "*As a* psychologist, I believe this category of citizens *should be* a 'protected class.'"

"I wear a suit when I'm arrested," commented Benjamin Spock, the famous pediatrician. "I think it helps to remind people that this (Vietnam protest) isn't a rowdy act but a carefully considered demonstration that *I deem worthy* of great respect."

Rousseau, one of the few romantics who did not join the intellectuals of his day, has sound advice for our misanthropic academics:

> Consider the danger of one stirring up the enormous masses which form the French nation. Who could restrain the disturbance set up, or foresee all

the results it might produce? Even if all the advantages of the new scheme should be indisputable, what man of good sense would dare to undertake to abolish old customs, to change old maxims, and to give a new form to a State other than that it has reached after an existence of 1,300 years?

My dear colleagues, or in Eric Hoffer's term, "men of words," why is not your vision more universal? Do you know the likely outcome of a continual exacerbation of American particularity in regards to race, class, gender, and sexual orientation? Where is your attention to the universals that knit us together? Our national motto, *e pluribus unum* ("out of many, one") has traditionally focused on *unum*,(unity), but you have shifted the focus to separateness, the particularity of many. The passionate trumpeting of externals is rapidly changing America from a melting pot to a "tossed salad," and ultimately to separate (and hostile) "salads." Where in your gospel of polarization are the bonds of empathy, collegiality, and understanding that enable us to see our nation as a unified whole and not as a collection of disconnected parts? Why have you left your high calling of mind-culture in favor of the divisive exacerbation of the volatile passions?

Intellectuals of the previous century provided the psychological tinder for igniting the Great War. Are today's intellectuals providing the seedbed for our nation's second Civil War? Benda claimed the intellectuals of his generation had blood on their hands even though they held no weapons, even though their boots had not been sullied by the muck of the trenches. If our generation of "academics of passion" keep up their rhetoric will they, too, accept responsibility for the fratricidal blood that may be shed in the next century?

The great 18th century English conservative, Edmund Burke, was not a moss-backed opponent of positive and necessary social change. He supported the American, Irish, and Indian Revolutions and one in his own country, the "Glorious Revolution of 1688." But in his classic work, *Reflections on the Revolution in France*, he noted that the passion unleashed by the Terror resulted in the ruthless, blind destruction of the existing order. Change that endures builds upon existing foundations rather than destroying them. He would advise intellectuals to:

> Approach the faults of the state as the wounds of a father, with pious awe and trembling solicitude. By this wise prejudice we are taught to look with horror on those children of their country who are prompt rashly to hack that aged parent in pieces and put him into the kettle of magicians, in hopes that by their poisonous weeds and wild incantations they may regenerate the paternal constitution and renovate their father's life.

A recent National History Standards proposal for all public schools, developed at the University of California at Los Angeles, is fraught with polarizing particularity. (The ideological pre-World War I intellectuals are redivivus in our time!) According to the proposal, American and world history are to be viewed primarily through the ideological prism of race, ethnicity, and gender. Lack of balance is pervasive. Positive words like "contribution," "accomplishment," and "achievement" are associated with non-Western far more frequently than with Western civilization. The UCLA academics cite the Great Depression 14 times, but one searches in vain for a mention of prosperity, liberty, and freedom. Scientific pioneers whose genius benefited all humankind--Thomas Edison, Alexander Graham Bell, the Wright Brothers, and others--are not mentioned. The name of Neil Armstrong, the first man on the moon, is absent from the new proposal for "historical standards."

Lynne V. Cheney, a member of the standards committee, drew up a list of what is trendy and fashionable in U.S. history:

WHAT'S "IN"	WHAT'S "OUT"
National Organization of Women	U.S. Marines
Seneca Falls (Gay) Declaration	Gettysburg Address
Watergate	D-Day
Richard Nixon	George Washington
Joseph McCarthy	Thomas Jefferson
Iran-Contra	Moon Landing
Ku Klux Klan	Federalist Papers
Diversity	Prosperity
Gender Roles	Liberty
American Indian Movement	Baptists

My advice for our academics? Return to the ivory tower both physically and symbolically. Leave passion and politics to the politicians. To become entangled in the public arena, from the town hall to international relations, is to be involved in a world of complexity that is infinitely beyond most academics' imagination. Of course, there are a select number of intellectuals--Henry Kissinger and Adlai Stevenson come to mind--who have made the transition from academe to politics with a modicum of success. But even those academics who are successful in the public arena should not allow *particularistic passions to either control or drive them.* It is easy to be a word-smith and propose solutions for man's intractable problems from the quiet of one's study. It is easy to be an academic know-it-all behind a lectern before a captive adolescent audience. It is quite another reality to enter the pressure chamber of contending interest groups and hammer out solutions that move incrementally toward the common good.

My dear academic colleagues, do not aspire to convert the souls of your students. Students in college should not be turned from their sunrise world of intellectualism to fanaticism. Strive instead to increase their individual intellectual, moral, and spiritual capital. Those forms of capital grow best in times of social harmony. Passion is the antithesis of mind-culture. Within months after Appomattox, General Robert E. Lee wrote that only "the allayment of passion, the dissipation of prejudice, and the restoration of reason" would reestablish the peace and harmony of the Union. Lee accepted the presidency of Washington and Lee College, while northern intellectuals and politicians continued to vent their spleen on the South for over a decade.

In *The Vision of the Anointed*, Thomas Sowell quotes Edmund Burke's statement that "barbarism is an ever-present threat when the civilizing institutions are weakened or undermined." Sowell adds:

> Civilization is not inherited; it has to be learned and earned by each generation anew; if the transmission should be interrupted for one century, civilization would die, and we should be savages again.

The fragility of civilization is real. Be wary, therefore, of social experimentation, grand designs, "new moralities," atomistic reasoning and your dreams, which Sowell calls, "the vision of the anointed." "The stock of reason in each man including yourself," states Burke, "is small, and individuals would do better to avail themselves of the general bank and capital of nations and of ages."

My dear colleagues, acknowledge that visions of cosmic justice are inevitably flawed by the Law of

Unintended Consequences. Concede that "the ideal is the enemy of the good" and substitute a tragic vision of life for utopian blueprints. Let not the acceptance of something positive--democratic diversity--lead to something problematic and potentially destructive-- undemocratic division and rigid factionalism.

Eschew the claim that politics is the most relevant theater of human intercourse. Remember the advice of the poet Robert Frost, who once said: "Don't join too many gangs. Join few if any. Join the United States and join the family--but not much in between unless a college." Refuse to be co-opted by political power, stay out of the streets, lower your voice, straight-jacket your rhetoric, and remember that the pen is mightier than the placard. Resist demonizing those who disagree with your ideological vision. Consider that many policies advanced today under the hallowed name of "diversity" might better be associated with a less agreeable word: "fragmentation." Refuse to label your opponents as greedy, racists, sexists, morally inferior, mentally deficient, or lacking in compassion. Remember Hamlet-- "Lay not that flattering unction to your soul."

This much is certain. Intellectuals will lose freedom if they continue to politicize from their protected oasis. Academics should endeavor to be more universal, generous, and humane; less narrow, polarizing, and relativistic. They should admit that there are intractable problems that no human intervention nor agency can repair *and* that they can't always distinguish those problems from the ones that *can* be fixed. We can dream of worlds we can never build. Tragedy is everywhere endemic; it is a condition that cannot be exorcised.

The State, unlike the Church, is not a redemptive community. Just as will power cannot cure an endocrine imbalance, neither can politics solve our endemic moral and spiritual afflictions. "How small, of all that human hearts endure," said Samuel Johnson, "that part which laws or kings can cause or cure."

Intellectuals should show greater appreciation of those who work in the marketplace, till the earth, create the goods, services and wealth and pay the taxes that sustain our collective enterprise. Honor those in blue and khaki who are fulfilling the first responsibility of the State, that of bringing order, both within and outside our nation. Finally, my dear and collegial intellectuals, may humility, a quality usually scarce within our guild, increase among us. Let us never forget that academia has often been the mid-wife of modern totalitarian movements. Most of the assassins of the leaders of democratic nations share three characteristics: They are students or ex-students, are ideologically driven, and are aflame with self-righteous passion. Such was Yigal Amir, the law student and murderer of Israel's Prime Minister Yitzhak Rabin.

Nineteen

Hiroshima, Truman, and Revisionist Historians

Fifty years ago President Truman made a decision that may have saved my life. Two sunbursts of nuclear energy over Japan during the torpid month of August foreclosed my becoming an active participant in the final stage of World War II. The order to rotate our squadron to Okinawa in September was canceled.

At the time there was near-universal rejoicing and support for Truman's decision to use the Atomic Bomb. Now, a half-century later, controversy continues to swirl around what I regarded then, and do now, to be a tragic but necessary decision.

The revisionist case has always been weak. It assumes that the atom-bombing killed a disproportionate number of civilians, that the Japanese were ready to surrender, that the bomb could have been dropped on an uninhabited atoll, that we were racists to use a nuclear weapon on non-Caucasians, or that our invasion of the Japanese islands would have been a cake-walk with few casualties. All such suppositions are a stretch. It is the revisionists who lack the 20-20 vision usually associated with hindsight. President Truman acted on the facts available to him and showed a remarkable clarity of vision and purpose.

First the issue of proportionality. The firebombing of Dresden on February 1945 killed the same number of people, 35,000, as did the atom-bombing of Nagasaki; in Hiroshima, 80,000 were killed. By contrast, the jellied gasoline attack on Tokyo by the U.S. 20th Air Force on March 9, 1945, resulted in 200,000 dead. All told, in the months before Hiroshima, bombs killed up to 500,000 in Japanese cities and left 13 million homeless. The atomic bomb was a hair-of-the-dog remedy--a last swig of slaughter to end the slaughter.

A recent release of declassified intercepts of Japanese diplomatic communications and the notes of the policy makers who advised Truman (Henry L. Stimson, Secretary of War; Cordell Hull, Secretary of State; Frank Knox, Secretary of the Navy; Admiral E. J. King, Chief of Naval Operations; General George Marshall, Army Chief of Staff) are clear regarding the following facts:

1. Joseph Stalin was never going to help the U.S. in its fight against Japan until Russia could profit from the move. Knowing this, Tokyo had secretly brought back hundreds of thousands of its troops from Manchuria to defend the home islands, leaving Manchuria and Korea easy prey for the Russians. When Truman told Stalin about our bomb at the Potsdam Conference in July 1945, the Soviet dictator greeted the news coolly and secretly ordered his minions to press harder on their own atom-bomb project.

Given the strides of physics, there was an inevitability about someone's using an A-bomb. If there had not been an American bomb, that would not have precluded an eventual Russian, German, or Japanese bomb. "You know Hiroshima has shaken the whole world," Stalin told his scientists at the end of the war. "The equilibrium has been destroyed. Provide the bomb--it will remove a great danger from us." Looking back, we were lucky. We won the race.

2. President Truman knew that the Japanese home islands were defended by 2.3 million troops. Another four million Japanese army and navy employees and a newly created militia numbering 28 million would also be armed. These defenders, like the kamikaze pilots who devastated our fleet off Okinawa, had sworn to fight to the death. Japanese troops had fought to the last man in battles throughout the Pacific. Would they do any less in defending the soil their Shinto religion considered sacred?

Because of Hiroshima, American troops would not be discharging their flame-throwers into caves and choking on the smell of gasoline and burning flesh. They would not have to do sweaty *pas de deux* with soldiers shouting "Banzai!" They would not be bayoneted, shot, or blown up by mines or mortars. The bomb was a reprieve made all the sweeter by its unexpectedness.

3. Many scientists felt the bomb would fizzle and be a dud. Others felt the yield would be on the low side, equal to about 200 tons of TNT. The following ditty was recited by some scientists as they awaited the explosion in New Mexico:

> From this crude lab that spawned a dud
> Their necks to Truman's ax uncurled
> Lo, the embattled savants stood
> And fired the flop heard 'round the world.

Had the bomb not worked, the air force would have had to continue to rain firebombs on Japanese cities until Tokyo surrendered. In the end, even more lives would have been sacrificed on both sides.

4. Our forces had suffered 30% to 35% casualties in invading Iwo Jima and Okinawa. On hearing of the

additional forces and fortifications by way of the intercepted Japanese communications, General MacArthur revised his pre-invasion needs for hospital beds by upwards of 300%. MacArthur's chief surgeon, General Guy Denit, estimated that a 120-day campaign to invade and occupy just the island of Kyushu would result in 395,000 casualties.

    5. Summaries of the intercepted messages reveal that, throughout June and July of 1945, Japan's militarist leaders were adamantly determined that they would never surrender unconditionally to the British and the Americans. The diehards preferred collective *hara-kiri*, national suicide, rather than surrender. "Would not it be wondrous for this whole nation," implored General Anami, the war minister, "to be destroyed like a beautiful flower?" While the Japanese military leaders knew they were beaten, historian Stanley Weintraub has indicated in *The Last Great Victory*, that they were far from ready to surrender. Their bitter-end slogan called for "the honorable death of a hundred million"--Japan's entire population.

    6. Immediately after the two atomic bombs were dropped, Russia invaded Manchuria and Mamoru Shigemitsu, the new foreign minister, began a propaganda campaign to brand the Americans as war criminals for using nuclear weapons. Tokyo's goals included keeping Emperor Hirohito from being tried for instigating a war of aggression, and diverting Western attention away from the legion of Japanese atrocities committed since the 1937 start of the Sino-Japanese war. "I think we should make every effort," Shigemitsu stated in September 15, 1945, "to exploit the atomic bomb question in our propaganda." That propaganda campaign has borne its final fruit 50 years later in the revisionist account of the bombing of Japan.

    7. The Samurai tradition--*Bushido*, the "Way of the Warrior"--added to the Confucian principle of

absolute loyalty to superiors plus the soldier's faith in the *kami* or spirits of the land, all combined to make quite predictable a collectively suicidal defense of the Japanese home islands. "Duty is weightier than a mountain," was the soldier's credo, "while death is lighter than a feather." The Japanese soldier admitted no higher authority than the Emperor. He lacked a transcendent moral authority comparable to God in the Judeo-Christian world view. "Right" and "wrong" were decided by what the group--or the Emperor--thought and did.

Bushido is the origin of the fanaticism that would have greeted our invasion of the home islands. The idea of the nobility of death in action that dominated the Imperial Army ethos through the Pacific War was still intact. "If someone should inquire of you concerning the spirit of the Japanese," was the *Bushido* motto, "point to the wild cherry blossom shining in the sun." Before entering battle many Japanese units repeated in unison the mantra, "I am the sword of the emperor and it will not be sheathed until I die." They had no word for "defeat," and their suicidal mind-set was summed up in the war song "Umi Yukaba," which, roughly translated, went:

> Across the sea,
> Corpses in the water,
> Across the mountain,
> Corpses heaped upon the field;
> I shall die only for the Emperor,
> I shall never look back.

John Keats' *They Fought Alone* is an account of how a heroic handful of Americans fought the Japanese in the occupied island of Mindanao. The book describes the few captured Japanese soldiers as having "blank eyes because their souls had fled." Japanese rarely surrendered. They were taught as schoolchildren that the Sun Goddess had ordered them to conquer the world for Her.

She would glorify those who died in battle. Those who surrendered would bring endless disgrace upon themselves, their ancestors, and on their relatives and children.

Keats told of a Japanese intelligence officer who had been captured. He could not return to Japan, the residence of God on earth, nor was there any place for him in the after world. He had done something for which there was no name, Keats continued, "he was worse than dead."

In this age of angst, Americans are especially tormented by a collective guilt complex. Psycho-historians and revisionist historians have a field day with their free-wheeling interpretations. In *Hiroshima: Why America Dropped the Atomic Bomb*, Ronald Takaki claims Truman was a racist, suffered from an inferiority complex, and was an insecure and inexperienced president. Simply put, Truman tried to prove he "was not a 'sissy.'" Robert Jay Lifton and Greg Mitchell take us into an even deeper wallow in national angst. We have maintained a half-century's denial over this "pointless apocalypse," they maintain, and they sweepingly conclude that we are alienated from our entire political process as a result.

Yet, the evidence is clear and compelling. The use of nuclear weapons to end World War II quickly and decisively prevented the death and maiming of hundreds of thousands of American soldiers, sailors, marines, and airmen. Without the bomb their number would have been added to the 20 million victims--civilians and war prisoners--who died at the hands of the Japanese from the 1930s to August of 1945.

My brother and I could have been among their number. The bomb also saved the lives of some 150,000 Allied prisoners of war (50,000 had already died since 1942 as the result of horrible abuses) and civilian detainees in Japanese hands. Under orders from Tokyo, the

POWs were to be beheaded, stabbed, shot, or otherwise slaughtered en masse at the moment the invasion of the home islands began. Above all, the bomb saved millions of Japanese from becoming casualties of our pre-invasion bombing and shelling, followed by the invasion and forcible occupation.

In an age of political correctness, egalitarianism, and cultural relativism, it may seem harsh to state that Japanese brutality was both different in degree and in kind from that of other nations in World War II. Yet, one out of every three POWs was killed or died under Japanese internment. This fact and its ramifications was suppressed and sanitized for 50 years. Recently the Australian historian, Gavan Daws, in *Prisoners of the Japanese* (1994), interviewed thousands of survivors and uncovered long-forgotten documents that reveal one of the most cruel legacies of that war. The tortures inflicted on civilian internees, POWs, and other Asians--men strung up over open flames, women dragged naked behind motorcycles, their vaginas and breasts attached to wires through which electric current was passed, babies skewered on bayonets, and the like--are almost unbelievable. Sometimes Japanese soldiers chopped the heads off their POWs without trial, for sport. Sometimes they forced other captives to watch.

In *The Railway Man*, Eric Lomax, a POW survivor of building the infamous "Bridge on the River Kwai," documents the torture of imprisonment and the half-century of subsequent psychological torment that proved even more disabling than his physical injuries. Daws' summary is shocking:

> The Japanese were not directly genocidal. They did not herd their white prisoners into gas chambers and burn their corpses in ovens. But they drove them toward mass death just the same. They beat them until they fell, then beat them for

falling, beat them until they bled, then beat them for bleeding. They denied them medical treatment. They starved them. When the International Red Cross sent food and medicine, the Japanese looted the shipments. They sacrificed prisoners in medical experiments. They watched them die by the tens of thousands from diseases of malnutrition like beriberi, pellagra, and scurvy, and from epidemic tropical diseases: malaria, dysentery, tropical ulcers, cholera. Those who survived could only look ahead to being worked to death. *If the war had lasted another year, there would not have been a POW left alive.*

We rightly view the devastation of Hiroshima with horror, but such events have happened in all epochs of history. The Assyrians destroyed every major city in their region several times over, with body counts far exceeding that at Hiroshima, and the 14th century Tarter conqueror Tamerlane made pyramids of the skulls of those destroyed in his westward march. All armies have at times violated the generally accepted codes of military behavior. Japanese torture, however, was often marked by a sick sexuality, and it was visited upon men, women, and children, sometimes for no reason other than idle whim. The record makes instructive reading for those who may not understand why America concluded that there was something different about the Imperial Japanese military.

After fifty years Japan still flails about, in contrast to Germany, in trying to come to terms with its wartime past. To the rest of the world, in particular its neighbors in East Asia, there is much for which to atone. Japanese commanders were uninhibitedly brutal to their prisoners of war and to their subject people in China, Korea, and Burma. For Company A of Janesville, Wisconsin, after one year in captivity, Daws reported it was 17.5 times more lethal to be a prisoner of the Japanese than to be fighting them. The Japanese did not let observers from neutral countries or the International Red Cross into POW internment camps. Many of the Red Cross food packets were looted before they were delivered to the prisoners. Japanese officers worked over 100,000 of POWs to death building the Thailand-Burma railway.

Japanese right-wingers still deny the Nanjing massacre of 1937-38, in which marauding troops slaughtered some 200,000 Chinese. Add to this Pearl Harbor, vicious medical experiments on POWs that are beginning to surface, the brutal occupation of Korea, the infamous Bataan death march, the tens of thousands of Chinese, Korean, Philippine, Malaysian, Indonesian, and Dutch "comfort women" forced into prostitution, and other atrocities whose mere description paralyzes the spirit and numbs the soul. None of it seems to elicit collective shame, let alone national repentance. The reluctance to apologize continues to skew Japan's relations with its neighbors and the West. (Readers interested in the rather gruesome details of Japanese torture of and experimentation on POWs in World War II can read about them in the recently published material of Professor Keiichi Tsuneishi, a Japanese historian of science. Tsuneishi documents what transpired at the infamous Unit 731 at Pignfan, on the outskirts of Harbin in China.)

Voltaire believed that history is a trick that the living play on the dead, the victors on the vanquished. In spite of his cynicism, there is, of course, a modicum of truth in his observation. But revisionists are neither in the existential moment of President Truman nor sensitive to the angst surrounding his tragic yet necessary decision. They simply have no way of understanding the ethos of 1945. A radical's Vietnamese prism is a poor lens through which to try to scrutinize and understand the world of 1945.

Was the atom bomb an act of vengeance? Veterans deny it, but it may have been. Some ethicists may call vengeance, "retributive justice," an elegant way of saying, "let the punishment fit the crime." Considering the infamy of Pearl Harbor, the Bataan march, and the many other violations of the Geneva Code and international protocols of military conduct, it is understandable why vengeance could well have been at least a partial motivating force.

Vengeance, retaliation, retribution, or requital, are part of the emotional process of closure. World War I ended before a shot was fired on German soil. Consequently, the Allies took out their unrequited animus against the Germans at the peace table. The horrendous reparations assessed at Versailles helped set the stage for World War II. The devastation and consequent final surrender of Japan in the Second World War, like that of Germany, handed history a rare luxury--an opportunity to rebuild on a clean psychological slate.

As an economic postscript 50 years after Hiroshima, evidence abounds from the economic arena of conflict rather than the military arena that the Japanese may indeed be a different kind of people. A geographic and ethnic insularity wrought from blood, soil, and their Shinto animism, makes them "in but not of" international culture. Many scholars believe the Japanese are still at war with us. Although a work of fiction, Michael Crichton's best seller, *Rising Sun* graphically details the truth of the Japanese motto, "Business is war." Books such as Peter Drucker's, *The New Realities*, Ezra Vogel's *Japan as Number One*, Karl van Wolferen's, *The Enigma of Japanese Power*, Paul Kennedy's *The Rise and Fall of the Great Powers*, and Chalmers Johnson's *MITI and the Japanese Miracle* make the case in a more scholarly and serious vein.

However, a recent study, *The 1940 System*, by Yukio Noguchi, economics professor at Tokyo's Hitotsubashi University, argues that Japan's rigidly regulated economy is not something deeply rooted in the national character, but is rather a fairly recent imposition. Noguchi traces the roots of the present system to the war mobilization effort and the importation of fascist ideas. Fascist ideology spread from Italy to Germany and Spain and even to Thailand and Argentina in the 1930s and early 1940s, when it seemed for a while that fascism was the wave of the future. State-engendered cooperation displaced market capitalism in those countries.

Confirming Friedrich Hayek's insight that statists of the right and left are brothers under the skin, Noguchi found that Japan's planning bureaucrats--the *kakushin kanryo*--studied New Deal reforms as well as fascist techniques. "For the Japanese economy, the war never ended," writes Noguchi, and he is pessimistic about the possibility of change. He believes that Douglas MacArthur's occupation advisers left much of Japan's wartime economic system intact because it made it easier for them to run things.

The baneful legacy of the 1940s will be difficult to exorcise. Vested interests are not the primary reason for socio-economic stasis. John Maynard Keynes held it is really people's rigid ways of thinking that prevent society from adapting. If alive today, Keynes' message to the Japanese people would be, "I have shown you the enemy, and it is you."

We are entering a world where the old rules no longer apply. The Japanese have invented a new kind of trade--adversarial trade, trade like war, trade intended to wipe out the competition--which we are now only beginning to understand. Foreign competition is negated through an iron triangle--corporations, banks, and government--of cooperation, if not outright collusion. The iron triangle supports research at two dozen "silicone valley" sites in industries that the Japanese have decided they want to dominate in the 21st century.

The conflict is over technology and trade policy. Industrial devastation exists in many European and North American countries. A century ago when Admiral Perry's American fleet steamed into Tokyo Bay and opened up the nation, Japan was still a feudal society. Change seemed essential if Japan was to have any hope of being a leading force in the world. Yet, signs abound that Japan, while a world force, is still feudal, suspicious, and insular.

Perhaps the devastation wrought by the nuclear bomb pales in its intensity when compared to the harm being done by present day Japanese economic warfare. The Japanese are not our industrial saviors. They are our competitors. It is a lesson we should not forget.

Twenty

Sociobiology: Is Violence Sown In Our Genes?

The third reason we are fighting (the first is to preserve liberties; the second, to defeat the Nazis) is because men like to fight. They always have and they always will. Some sophists and other crackpots deny that. They don't know what they're talking about. They are either goddammed fools or cowards, or both. Men like to fight, and if they don't, they're not real men.

General George S. Patton, Jr.

Why do men go to war? Because the women are watching.

David Barash

In the late 1970s, Sociobiology, a new evolutionary synthesis, was a biological bombshell tossed into trenches of the humanities and social scientists. Its advocates stated that, whereas Darwin had shown our morphological connection with "lower" forms of life, recent research proved that a genetic influence also linked our behavior with other forms of animal life.

Science has always been a threat to assumptions of *Homo sapiens'* uniqueness and dignity. Galileo began with a cosmic, solar plexus punch that knocked us from our perch near the center of the universe. Newton's mechanistic world view caused many to wonder if they could still believe in a personal Deity. Darwin found in the fossil record that our origins reside in "lower" life forms of hundreds of thousands of years ago. If our roots come from some "primordial soup" rather than a Genesis-recorded, creative act of God, where then is the source of our spiritual uniqueness?

Finally, Freud and Skinner presumably destroyed our final presumptions of rationality, uniqueness, freedom, and dignity. The urges of the Id control our mental processes. Drives and forces--internal and external puppet strings--determine choices that we can neither comprehend nor remember. We live off the emotional programs laid down by our parents, teachers and our childhood traumas. In sum, our vaunted power of reasoning is but rationalizing. Our acts of love, duty and sacrifice are controlled by an invisible puppet master we can neither feel nor see.

Behavioral science has convinced us that however we play our role in life, we seldom know who the playwright is as we move robot-like across the stage. Our only succor is to allow psychiatrists to replace our priests and let them mediate secular revelations as to the etiology of our angst. The couch replaces the confessional booth. Absolution that used to be mediated gratis is now psychic integration that comes at $200 an hour. How sad it is. Freedom is but the knowledge of our determined past. We face, therefore, a terribly constricted future. We are but stimulus-response mechanisms--Pavlov's dogs with a human face.

The Greco-Christian worldview, the Scale of Being, that placed *Homo sapiens* at the summit of creation is about gone. The loss of a hierarchic universe increased our doubts as to whether we possessed an *imago Dei* linked to the Transcendent.

Science, it seems, has given communities of faith one body blow after another. But each time, man gets up from the canvas before the count of ten. Surprisingly, he persists in doing things science has told him to unlearn. He continues to drop to his knees, make the sign of the cross, honors some symbol, folds his hands, prays to God or an anti-god, performs a mitzvah, and gives his life over to an Ultimate Concern. *Homo sapiens'* religiosity is as indigenous to his nature as sexual intercourse.

Religion, faith, and belief in the Transcendent continue to inform human existence because science can never provide the ultimate meaning for the human condition. Nor can it be the *Mysterium Tremendum* that empowers, ennobles, loves, and forgives. Paul Tillich held that authentic faith always has an "in spite of" element. Life, it seems, is more than logic. As Pascal observed, "The heart has its reasons of which the mind knows not." As our century closes, evidence exists that concern for the spiritual is growing in both its authentic and its idolatrous expression. Across our globe religious movements, both the fanatic and the sane, are on the make. Rival scientific schools have spread-eagled human nature in a tug of war from "below" and from "above." One school has "lifted" certain animals up to the level of humans. Research has indicated dolphins, whales, and chimpanzees are sentient and may be capable of thought. The other school pulls us back into the evolutionary mists from which we thought we had risen. It holds that behaviorally, for all our vaunted spirituality and rationality, we are nothing more than a naked ape.

Now, a new threat is about to become troublesome to both the faithful and the behaviorists. Behaviorism, recently the dominant ideology in psychology--the self is but a lump of plastic that was molded by the environment--has come under heavy attack by the Sociobiologists. Sociobiology claims that genes code more than our physiological inheritance; indeed, genes influence behavior. Whereas Freud held that our behavior is determined by an emotional program laid down by our parents during our childhood, Sociobiologists believe our behavior has been shaped by the eons of evolution.

It may be time for a new paradigm of human behavior. Liberal and progressive hope for a utopia by way of social engineering and conditioning is at dead end. As we enter the 21st century, we are disillusioned over failed educational, social and environmental experiments to alter social behavior. America has spent trillions of dollars on welfare, education, Head Start, penology, and other forms of social amelioration. Yet, rage, violence, homicide, rape, social pathology and incivility continue to rise. Researchers and scholars can write the blueprints for *Walden II*, but they cannot replicate it. Even religious communes sometimes end in a communion of poison-laced grape Kool Aid or in a Texas firestorm.

As we close out the second millennium, Americans are a chastened people. We cannot change our nature even if we exert our will, reshape our neighborhoods, pick up the garbage, grant Head Start to all, and pass the most benevolent of laws. Man is not his own maker, fashioner, or improver. We are part of, not separate from, the mysterious and complex life forms on the planet. Sociobiology affirms that evolution is still king. Genetic selfishness is not pathological. A mother ewe will drive off an orphan lamb because, if she allowed it to nurse, she would not have enough milk for her own offspring. Sociobiologists claim the altruism we show for members of our tribe can be traced precisely to the genetic connections we have with one another.

According to Konrad Lorenz, "the Great Constructors"--Aggression, Flight, Feeding and Reproduction--have shaped us as they have the eagle, the walleye, the butterfly, and the whale. Many male traits, such as aggressiveness and hyperactivity, were useful millennia ago when there were woolly mammoths to be hunted, or even centuries ago during the Thirty Years' War. But the Stone Age and the Middle Ages are long gone and such traits are ruinous in todays' cities. The damage Stone Age, club-wielding Hitlers or Sadams could do was microscopic compared to the havoc caused by their technologically armed descendents today.

Wherever a behavior pattern is universal in diverse cultures, a genetic factor is presumed to be involved. Patriarchy, nepotism, homosexuality, aggression, territoriality, dominance, kin selection, altruism, sexual roles, hypergamy, exogamy, incest taboos, and sex-based infanticide are among the behavioral uniformities that exist amid all the cultural richness and diversity of our world. Anthropologists, in focusing on the differences between societies, tend to look at the icing, while ignoring the cake that lies underneath. Yet that behavioral "cake" is remarkably constant among all peoples. Then too, the behavioral conformity of identical twins separated at birth and raised in completely different environments is astounding. Obviously, correspondence does not necessarily mean causation. Yet, similarity in choices such as rings, food, music, sport, hair style, and other interests seems explainable only in terms of genetic predisposition.

The basic argument is simple and clear. Man is a complex primate, physiologically still geared to be a hunter and gatherer. Now forced to live in an artificial world created by modern technology, he bears the genes of a primordial past. A division of labor separated men into the hunters, women into the gatherers. This divergence was non-sexist and egalitarian. Each gender bonded and honed the skills unique to its vocation. Each educated its own and passed such knowledge and skills down to the next generation. The vocation of each gender was needed for genetic success, that is, getting the necessary genes into the next generation. The Taoist symbol of Yin-Yang reveals that reality is made up of dualities such as heat and cold, male and female. They are in complementary rather than opposite relationships.

Sociobiologists are divided between those who contend we are "hard-wired" (genetic determinists) and those who see us as "soft-wired" (genetic influence advocates, who allow a larger role for culture). The genetic determinists see a human life as a bullet shot from a gun: it goes where it's aimed and has no choice in the matter. The metaphor used by the "soft-wired" advocates is that of a genetic paper airplane thrown into an environmental wind. A "hard-wired" explanation of Eskimo geriatric suicide during a harsh winter is that such altruism is a genetic compulsion to husband scarce resources for the young. Proponents of the "soft-wired" theory have a different explanation: while not discounting all genetic stimulus, they believe that culture--stories and tribal teachings told to youth about the heroic sacrifice of elders-- socializes the elderly to step onto the ice flow or to leave camp during a blizzard.

The attack on Sociobiologists by Marxists, feminists, behaviorists, and liberals has been unrelenting. When David Barash, author of *The Whisperings Within*, lectured at Hamline University in the late 70s, he had to run a gauntlet of blacks, feminists, and Marxists who protested and placarded his visit. His liberal, non-establishment appearance--long hair, beard, turtle-neck pullover, leather-elbowed sport jacket did not protect him from their venom. Sociobiology, nevertheless, is not reductionistic but inclusive. It wants to upgrade social science, not bury it. The controversy seems to prove, however, that scientists are just as subjective and prone to bias as the rest of us. Scientists, too, tend to resist new ideas, any new ideas, often for no other apparent reason than because anything new must conflict with whatever they had previously been taught. With the passage of time, they will lose. "A new scientific truth does not triumph by convincing its opponents and making them see the light," wrote the great physicist, Max Planck, "but rather because its opponents eventually die, and a new generation grows up that is familiar with it."

The central question is: "Can man survive his nature?" Reinhold Niebuhr brought a necessary correction to the anthropology of theological liberals by putting forth a new appreciation and interpretation of original sin. Sociobiology is performing the same service for social science by interjecting a needed realism, perhaps even pessimism, into the discussion.

Our ancestors successfully mastered the non-human environment and then shifted their warrior attentions to other tribes. Like our urban gangs today, those with the best organization, attack, and defensive skills survived. We are threatened today, however, with social anarchy, perhaps even extinction, because our greatest gifts--intelligence and dexterity--are a mixed blessing. Of all the animal world we have no claws, beak, or great teeth. In spite of health clubs, Stair-Masters, and Nordic Tracks, our running, swimming, climbing, and endurance capabilities are modest compared to those of many animals. Our technological capability for destruction, however, has grown exponentially--from stones, sticks, arrows, swords, cross-bows, rifles, bombs--to nuclear and bacteriological instruments. Tragically, unlike animals, we have few genetic inhibitory mechanisms and rituals that prevent the killing of our own kind.

When I took Pepper, our small mongrel dog, for a walk she was often attacked by a neighbor's Labrador. Invariably, Pepper would roll on her back, thrust up her paws, and bare her throat to her attacker. Pepper's genetic trigger telegraphed the message--"You are bigger than I am, victory is yours, I submit." The Labrador accepted the symbolic triumph. Instantly the attack stopped, tails would wag, and the dogs would sniff each other. Neither was injured by the other's innate aggression. Without such symbolic appeasement, intra-species aggression would go beyond working for the optimum fitness of each species and threaten its very survival.

Holocausts, however, are unique to *Homo sapiens*. We are the only species that indulges in the mass slaughter of its own kind.

Suggestions on how to control our intra-species fighting instinct are many. Theoretically, eugenics could breed out violence once the gene responsible for aggression was located. But aggression might be the core of personality and, like anxiety, necessary to personal achievement as well as creative expression. Self-knowledge regarding our innate violence might be helpful so that with sublimation, anti-social drives might be reduced by means of throwing cheap crockery or other forms of catharsis. A regimen of sports competition might reduce the violence between street gangs over their respective turfs. Competition by couch-potatoes to improve the environment might reduce their violence against spouses and children. Expanding Olympics and international competition might increase international contact and friendship. Dedication to international dilemmas and problems in medicine, the environment, the arts, science, even humor might play a part in releasing tension and unmasking our pretensions.

Critics of this biologized view of man maintain that our large brain shows our behavior is not genetically determined. While violence, patriarchy, sexism and nastiness certainly have biological urgings, so too do peacefulness, equality, beneficence, and love reveal a genetic influence; we are able to make choices as to which stirrings we'll obey. Nurturists claim we should listen to the more noble stirrings of our angelic nature and strengthen such impulses. This much is certain--the controversy, as part of the classic nature/nurture debate, will continue into the future. If the 21st century proves *Homo sapiens* to be more humane and generous than did the bloody century we are about to exit, Sociobiology may be forced into seclusion.

Those who have studied the decisions of the Supreme Court maintain that, however abstract the judges' jurisprudence and logic, their decisions are often influenced by the latest elections. In like fashion, abstract musings regarding the nature and behavior of *Homo sapiens*, are conditioned by what is happening in the ghetto and in the school, at home and on the battlefield. Bloody times, simply put, generate seemingly brutal theories.

It would be wrong, I believe, to only see *Homo sapiens* through the "bloody tooth and claw" genetic prism. Our nature, as Pascal wisely saw, is composite, mysterious, and dialectical.

> What a chimera then is man! What a novelty! What a monster, what a chaos, what a contradiction, what a prodigy! Judge of all things, imbecile worm of the earth; depositary of truth, a sink of uncertainty and error; the pride and refuse of the universe!

I agree with Pascal that it is dangerous to make man see his "equality with the brutes without showing him his greatness. It is also dangerous to make him see his greatness too clearly, apart from his vileness." Indeed, we are worse than the brute since, when its stomach is full it slumbers and its killing ceases. Let us never think that we are *either* entirely brutish or angelic. We are both. "Man is but a reed," according to Pascal, "the most feeble thing in nature; but he is a *thinking* reed."

In sum, let us discover the mysterious urges of our genes. The Human Genome Project should go forward. It promises freedom to legions of those who suffer from inherited genetic afflictions. But let us also hear the higher angelic voices of our nature. They call us to supranatural obligations of love, nobility, sacrifice, and heroism.

Twenty One

The Churches' Failure Of Moral Guidance During Desert Storm

I went to a Catholic Field Mass where all of us were armed. As we knelt in the mud in the slight drizzle, we could distinctly hear the roar of the guns, and the whole sky was filled with airplanes on their missions of destruction... quite at variance with the teachings of the religion we were practicing.

General George S. Patton, Jr. on his Sunday in Normandy in World War II

Beware the people who moralize about great issues; moralizing is easier than facing hard facts.

John Corry

When President Bush agonized over whether to put a coalition of forces into combat to fulfill the mandate of the United Nations Security Council and Congress, he sought guidance from the Reverend Edmund Browning, the presiding bishop of the Episcopal Church. "War is not an option that would serve anyone," was the cleric's response.

"I wish the bishop would read the 84 page Amnesty International report on the rape of Kuwait," Bush later remarked, "and then tell me what to do!"

Subsequently, the president turned to Billy Graham. This shift in focus from a Mainline bishop to one of our most popular evangelical pastors mirrored a significant change in American religious loyalty.

In the fifth century, as the Roman Empire was collapsing, Saint Augustine set forth the seven criteria for the *justum bellum*, the just war. The followers of Jesus of Nazareth had evolved from an ascetic, world-denying sect to a powerful church and had entered public and social life. The predicted Second Coming and the end of history had not come to pass; consequently, the Church had to take responsibility for its age. Christians needed guidance regarding the legitimate use of coercion. Eschewing the extremes of pacifism and the *jihad*, Augustine set forth the criteria for the just yet "mournful and tragic" war. Those criteria--defensive resistance, last resort, worthy cause, and proper authorization, together with proper attitude, proportional force, and relative safety of noncombatants--have been the moral frame for the Western approach to war for fifteen centuries.

Augustine knew, as did most major theologians who followed him, that the world could be ruled neither by moral homily nor by ecclesiastical fiat. Regarding Desert Storm, it now appears that most Mainline (critics use the term "Oldline" or "Sideline") Protestant and a few Catholic leaders repudiated that classic moral tradition. In so doing, they betray short memories. In an early 1930s poll, Harry Emerson Fosdick, the religious spokesman of his era, asked 19,372 Protestant clergymen, "Do you believe the churches of America should now go on record as refusing to sanction or support any future war?" Sixty-two percent answered, "Yes." When Douglas MacArthur took issue with their judgment, Harold E. Fey, a leading religion editor, said the General sounded like Kaiser Wilhelm.

Mainline churches are still prone to the antimilitary hyperbole engendered by Vietnam. Like generals who, it is claimed are always fighting a past war, Mainline antiwar activists opposed the Persian Gulf war in terms of Vietnam, even in situations where the comparison was totally inapplicable.

Protestant churches have attempted to expunge war and military terminology from their hymnals--this even though the Old and New Testaments are full of military metaphors for the spiritual and moral engagements of life. Several years ago, the United Methodists were forced to restore "Onward Christian Soldiers" and "The Battle Hymn of the Republic" to their new hymnal because of thousands of letters of protest to the selection committee.

The churches that opposed Desert Storm invariably substituted sentiment for moral analysis. Editorials in Mainline publications were replete with the horror and "obscenity of war," dwelling on its wastage of blood and money. In January 1991, the leaders of more than twenty denominations spoke of doomsday scenarios--a victory over Iraq would produce "no winners" and would "unleash violence that would only multiply and reverberate" for generations. They asked that churches support and give sanctuary to those soldiers who discovered they were conscientious objectors. The covenants that soldiers have with the military, it seemed, were not as important as those made in business or the church.

A moralism that holds war to be an unalloyed evil prevents judicious reasoning. The night of war is so dark that one cannot distinguish between cats, be they black or white. Moreover, Mainline leaders have repudiated the advice of one of their own, Reinhold Niebuhr: If a "season of violence" can overthrow tyranny and establish a more just social system, he reflected, "there is no purely ethical ground upon which violence and revolution can be ruled out."

The fast-growing evangelical churches (which some Mainliners hold in low regard) overwhelmingly supported the action to liberate Kuwait. "If a call for cease-fire was put to a vote of the membership of the National Council of Churches, it would lose, and lose badly," remarked Richard Land of the Southern Baptist Convention's Christian Life Commission.

Mainliners substituted tangential issues to avoid the fundamental question, "How should Saddam Hussein be stopped?" Some lamented our addiction to oil, asserting that Bush wanted a war to bring the economy out of recession. Others resorted to pop psychology, opining that war is "mass murder" and that we are addicted to a Rambo "bully-on-the-block" identity. Historic reasons for the conflict were advanced (it came about because the Ottoman Empire was improperly carved up after World War II) as were sociological ones (it revealed our hatred of Arab peoples). Some even suggested that if Sadam did not exist we would have to invent him because the American psyche must define itself by an "omnipresent enemy" rather than by ideals.

The naiveté of those commenting on the geopolitical issues regarding the Middle East was astounding. Sometimes Mainliners tried to be cute. James Wall, editor of *The Christian Century*, opined that "if Kuwait's major export were Brussels sprouts our reaction would have been far less vigorous."

A century after Frederick Douglass pleaded with Abraham Lincoln to let blacks share the Union's military burden, many Mainliners joined Coretta Scott King, Jesse Jackson, and other pillars of the civil rights establishment in complaining that blacks bear too much of it. Although blacks are 12 percent of America's population, they represented 20 percent of Desert Storm personnel. Yet, such was Mainliner hatred for the military that they repudiated the draft, the only effective means of bringing equity, by balancing responsibility and rights among all groups in defense of freedom.

Mainliners overlook the fact that the military's level playing field, symbolized by retired General Colin Powell, former chairman of the Joint Chiefs, has itself proved to be particularly attractive to blacks simply by rewarding merit, not race. "Where else," asks Charles Moskos, military sociology professor at Northwestern University, "does a young black man know that, with a little hard work, he can earn the opportunity to yell orders at young white men?"

Sadly, Desert Storm increased the alienation between Mainline Christians and Jews. Saddam often used Holocaust metaphors in promising to "incinerate" and "obliterate" Israel. His Scuds forced a people who had lost six million in the death camps to put on gas masks and be confined to sealed rooms. Mainliners seem dead to such images. "Some Protestant and Catholic leaders," commented Steven Derfler, former professor of Jewish Studies at Hamline University, "do not care whether Israel survives or not." Five years after Desert Storm, with the United Nations oil embargo finally beginning to take effect, Saddam finally admitted that Iraq had been on the brink of developing nuclear weapons and had tons of bacteriological agents.

Because they make their living from the oral word, Mainline pastors have overemphasized the power of moral suasion as the solvent of national egoism. Ruthless tyrants with no compunction about bloodshed always play on religious idealists' revulsion toward war. The churches' agony over war is their badge of moral authority. Their moral sentimentalism, however, is converted by brutal dictators to their own ends. A peace gained by war is not a perfect peace, but it certainly is a better peace than that maintained by tyranny.

A "soft" utopianism that minimizes or ignores the dangers of predatory collective egoism, I believe, may be every bit as responsible for despotism as the "hard" utopianism of Marxism or Fascism.

The Seventh Assembly of the World Council of Churches (WCC), which met in Canberra, Australia, during the bombing phase of the Persian War, released a highly charged position paper titled, "Stop the War! Pursue the Way of Peace!" The Assembly narrowly avoided accepting a radical amendment that called upon churches to reject all "theological and moral justification for the use of military power," a resolution that would have put the WCC on record as being a pacifist organization. The document was anti-American and anticoalition in tone. "Some of us have been increasingly concerned that the WCC is trying to occupy a moral ground so unworldly and perfectionist that it won't be listened to by the real world," commented a delegate from the Church of Scotland.

"Peace with Justice" has been the slogan of the Mainline for several decades. But where is the biblical and democratic value of freedom? A January 1991 statement on the Gulf crisis issued by the council of bishops of the United Methodist church and read in all pulpits made no mention of concern for the ravished people of Kuwait. Later, when it was brought to his attention, the president of the council said it had been an "unfortunate oversight."

Evangelical Protestants tend to speak out of love regarding our failures as a nation. Mainliner statements, perhaps influenced by liberation theology, tend to be weighted with guilt. The National Council of Churches, for example, asked that the celebration of the quincentennial of Columbus' discovery of America focus on repentance for starting "centuries of genocide." Totally missing was the romance that tens of millions of common men, the "garbage of Europe" (and scores of other regions), in Eric Hoffer's words, have had with the American Experiment. Mainline pronouncements, therefore, are too often undialectical, unnuanced, harsh, and need more subtlety.

Sociologically, what this means is that Protestant churches are increasingly speaking as sects. They covet the prestige that comes with membership and power but are increasingly behaving like Quakers, River Brethren, Mennonites, and Amish. They have forfeited an Augustinian prudential analysis of the moral criteria of regarding violence. Churches by definition are inclusive; they adjust and accommodate to the values of culture. Churches accept the constraints that sin and the will to power place on the reformation of human nature and national communities. Historically, church adjudicators have had their feet firmly planted on the terra firma of the possible. They have not allowed the blue sky fancies of the impossible and the preachments of the zealots to override their worldly prudence. Churches work within the dialectic of the "impossible possibility" and do not sacrifice "eternity to time" by assuming utopias can be historic possibilities.

Given these limits, they work for incremental, proximate goals of human betterment. Nor do churches destroy the myths, values, and traditions that serve as the glue that binds a people together. Sects, on the other hand, are communities of the alienated. By nature exclusive, judgmental, angry, and passionate, they seek psychic if not geographical separation from the demonic culture within which they exist. Sects wish to be pure lights in an ever-darkening world. They denounce more than they affirm. Sects speak in accents of the sociopolitical "wilderness" while churches connect to main street and the marketplace. Churches are nurtured by chaplains. Sects create iconoclasts. Churches seek consensus and can compromise, whereas the zeal for purity of a sect means it will always be a remnant.

Protestant evangelicals, on the other hand, are showing amazing vitality and growth. By using marketing strategies, the evangelicals are creating megachurches of up to fifteen thousand members. They create a sense of belonging through Bible study, prayer, and experiential religion. Evangelicals wave the flag, shed tears, and choke up while repeating the Pledge of Allegiance. Their values--law and order, love of country, the traditional family, sexual chastity, hatred of pornography, traditional gender roles, vouchers, public schools that allow prayer and are held accountable, limited government, and a market economy--are rock solid. Evangelicals repudiate much of the social agenda of the Mainline--ordination and marriage of homosexuals, Statism, "blame America first," "comparable worth," hiring quotas, and expanded entitlements. They believe such programs are tangential to the mission of the followers of Jesus.

The Gospel for the evangelicals is neither the furtherance nor acceptance of a program of political correctness.

Of course, there is nothing wrong with being a sect. God may not be with the majority, *vox populi, vox Dei* is a dangerous assumption. Small, disciplined groups have often shaped the course of history. Historically, most churches have started out as sects and evolved into churches by aculturating to societal values. Protestant Mainline churches, however, cannot have it both ways. They cannot denigrate the values of their members by speaking in sectist terms, yet expect their members to support the churches' institutional commitments.

The Mainline faces a problematic future. The separation between pulpit and pew, and the erosion of membership, status, and influence continue. Mainline church leadership may be right in thinking that the American Experiment is sick unto death and that responsible Christians should become cultural despisers who enter, for a time, the sectist wilderness. If that is their position, they should make it clear to the laity who serve, listen, and pay the bill. This much is sure: church leaders who wish to maintain their institutional strength, membership, and commitments should be wary of extremist and maladroit pronouncements more congenial to otherworldly sects. If such trends continue, the Mainline will continue its sad journey to the sideline.

Conclusion

Si vis pacem, para bellum
("If you want peace, prepare for war")

Flavius Vegetius, Roman military philosopher

If history teaches us anything it is that "Peace does not keep itself." According to Thucydides, people wage war because honor, fear, or self-interest seem to demand it. While we can understand the latter two, "honor" seems more difficult. For many in our generation, the word has an archaic ring. Perhaps honor has a more acceptable connotation regarding war if we render it as esteem, worth, integrity, character, prestige, or self-respect.

Every generation at some point has the utopian dream that somehow the god of war, Ares, will finally be enchained. In 1944 when a "visiting fireman of great eminence" told General George Patton that World War II would be the last war ever fought, Patton responded heatedly: "Such statements since 2600 B.C. have signed the death warrant of millions of young men. My God! Will they never learn?"

In 1910, *The Great Illusion*, by Norman Angell, purportedly proved that war was impossible. By impressive examples and incontrovertible argument, Angell showed that with Europe's present financial and economic interdependence, the victor would suffer equally with the vanquished; therefore war had become unprofitable. Ergo, no nation would be so foolish as to start one. Translated into dozens of languages, the gospel of *The Great Illusion* spread like a wildfire and generated a cult. Study groups populated by true believers and propagating its dogma popped up at the universities all across Europe.

Angell's most earnest disciple was a man with great influence on British military policy, the King's friend and adviser, Viscount Esher, chairman of the War Committee. Esher gave lectures at Cambridge, the Sorbonne and before the ranking military officers of both England and France, arguing that "new economic factors clearly prove the inanity of aggressive wars." The interlacing of nations is so "pregnant with restraining influences" as to make war "unthinkable and impossible."

Glory! Glory! Peace does not need keeping!

Lord Esher felt Germany would be as receptive as Britain and France to Angell's new revelation and thus gave copies of *The Great Illusion* to the Kaiser and the Crown Prince. History is mute regarding their reaction. In retrospect we know that, schooled in Clausewitz's precept--"The heart of France lies between Brussels and Paris"--they, together with their military junta, were perfecting General Alfred von Schlieffen's plan to invade Belgium and France.

Within a few years of the publication of *The Great Illusion*, the great battles of the Marne, Somme, Ypres, Chateau Thierry, and others had killed an entire generation of French, German, and British young men.

Two decades later, "peace," again, "did not keep itself." Tragically, dreams are more captivating and intoxicating than is the harsh reality of military sufficiency. Had the allies responded with force in 1936 when Hitler marched into the Rhineland and began rebuilding the Wehrmacht, the Nazi incubus would have been stillborn. In 1928, when I was two years old, 64 nations of the world (including Germany, Japan, and Italy) signed the infamous Kellogg-Briand Peace Pact. The signatories promised to *"Abolish War As An Instrument of National Conflict!"* Newspaper headlines around the world screamed--"War Is Outlawed," "Peace Now and Forever More," "Everlasting Peace in Our Time," "The War to End All War Was Not Fought In Vain." Church bells tolled the joyous news thoughout the West. The lion and the lamb would feed together. The great powers began to sink their warships and melt down their tanks and artillery. The Biblical dream would become a reality--we would turn "swords into plowshares and spears into pruning hooks." The locus of war was not in the heart of man but in its horrid armaments.

United States Secretary of State Franklin Kellogg received the 1929 Nobel Peace Prize for his efforts in creating the Pact. Henry Stimson said this piece of parchment would protect against aggression by "the sanction of public opinion, which can be made one of the most potent sanctions in the world. Critics who scoff at it have not accurately appraised the evolution in world opinion since the Great War." This staggering faith in world opinion, idealism, reason, and dialogue ended not just in tragedy but in parody: Idaho Republican Senator William Borah, upon hearing that war had broken out in Europe in September 1939, said, *"Lord, if only I could have talked with Hitler, all this might have been avoided."*

Is it not strange that there appears in every generation the persistent belief in the awesome power of parchment to keep the peace?

While the leaders of the Great Powers were signing parchments of peace, an anti-Semitic, frustrated, unemployed artist and veteran of the Great War was wandering the streets of Vienna and Munich. Later in jail, he set pen to parchment that contained quite a different message. The outcome was <u>Mein Kampf</u>.

The great misfortune in the 1920s and 1930s was that both France and England lacked leaders wise enough to move against the pacifist current. The Conservative prime minister, Stanley Baldwin, was a kindly, patient, and genuinely virtuous man who hated anything that smacked of confrontation. His favorite mood, according to a biographer, was "one of a sunset calm and nostalgia, in which the British nation, like an old couple in retirement enjoying the peaceful ending of the day, contemplated some sweep of English landscape and harkened to the distant church bells." Plagued by the memory of what it had endured in World War I, Britain wanted to hang on to what it had without fighting. Left or Right, everyone was for the quiet life.

Yet, in the pre-Victorian era, Britain's leaders had been ruthless strategists--tough, skeptical, and suspicious, ready to fight with swords, pistols, or fists. The hard, not soft virtues, had created "Rule Britannia." For over 200 years Britain had lived by a truism written by one of its own, Thomas Hobbes--"Covenants without swords are but words." But in the 1930s, the steely British backbone had been replaced by pasta. Blinded by its own virtues--gentleness, breeding, manners, compromise, compassion, idealism--Britain was soft and ripe. A wag opined that her approach to diplomacy was rather like the English approach to sex--"Romantically remote from the distressing biological crudities".

Appeasement can only be effective when applied from a position of strength, when it is a freely taken action meant to allay a grievance and create good will. It is a dangerous device when it is resorted to out of fear or necessity, for then it does not reduce resentment but shows weakness and instills contempt.

Hailed as a man of peace, Neville Chamberlain followed a policy of appeasement that was applied from a position of cravenness, not strength. *He was the all-too-familiar peacemaker who encourages war.* Motivated by the highest ideals, he nonetheless lacked the will to realize them. "In spite of the hardness and ruthlessness I thought I saw in Hitler's face," he wrote his sister after Munich, "I got the impression that *here was a man who could be relied on when he had given his word.*" After his monstrous error in judgment and his subsequent heartfelt invocation--"I believe it is peace for our time!"--the delighted crowds outside 10 Downing Street sang, "For he's a jolly good fellow." Britain had slipped into a collective and extensive denial.

Chamberlain had regarded Hitler and Mussolini as rational men like himself, with limited goals, who could be dealt with by flexibility and reasoned discussion. Chamberlain was the kind of man Theodore Roosevelt had in mind when he referred to William Howard Taft as one "who means well feebly."

Winston Churchill, in contrast, had two things Chamberlain lacked: the sagacity to understand the nature of the Nazi threat, and the gumption to oppose it tooth and claw.

As Churchill himself put it before the House of Commons in 1938, the British people had before them the choice of shame or war. He feared that they would choose shame--and have war nevertheless. He was right.

The French, too, were senseless beyond comprehension. Like the British, they had learned nothing from losing an entire generation of men in the flower of their youth a few years earlier. France relied on the Maginot Line, a perfect emblem of Gaelic military fatuousness. Neither France nor England deployed a credible offensive force. Western leaders examined their situation sentimentally and hopefully rather than objectively and realistically. They were moved by the horror of war, the fear of its reappearance, and the blind hope that a refusal to contemplate war and prepare for it would somehow keep the peace.

Contemporary literature joins recent history in warning us against complacency. Albert Camus' greatest work, *The Plague*, ends with an admonition. As the novel concludes, the pestilence that gripped Oran has finally run its course and the rats bearing their plague bacillus have retreated to their underground bunkers. But a final victory "against terror and its relentless onslaughts" is not to be. As Rieux, the heroic if absurdist existentialist physician, listens to the shouts of joy, "he knew what those jubilant crowds did not know but could have learned from books... *The plague... bides its time... and that the day would come when, for the bane and the enlightening of men, it would rouse up its rats again and send them forth to die.*"

Modern antibiotics can easily exterminate pestilences spread by bacteria. Camus, a French freedom fighter against the Nazi bacillus, did not intend us to take literally his figure of speech. Scourges and terrors mutate and recycle in hideous shapes and forms throughout history. The future is bleak but, in times of plague, I agree with Camus that it is comforting to know "there are more things to admire in men than to despise."

In spite of the passing of the Cold War era, the world is more and more a tangle of scourges. Tribal, ethnic, and ideological enmities are exploding across the continents like the naval salvos off the Normandy beaches during D Day. The notion that peace is natural and war an aberration has led to a failure in peacetime to consider the possibility of another war. Creating pacifist "peace studies" institutes and sanitizing the Bible and hymns of images of war has nothing to do with creating a statecraft that maintains world order. We must never forget the military proverb that the enemies within a city's walls, well meaning though they be, are ten times more dangerous than armies in the field and on the move.

Refusing to allow little boys to play cops and robbers or have G.I. Joe playthings as an antidote to aggression and war is fatuous and dim-witted. The causes of war are not to be found in the sandboxes of children, but rather in places where the power of predatory collectives is unchecked by vigorous and corresponding constraint.

"History is creative," according to Niebuhr, "but not redemptive." Neither the structure of nations nor the nature of man discloses a moral mutation toward altruism in our post-Cold War world. From the Peloponesian Wars to the present, the history of conflict teaches us one central lesson--a system of peace depends upon a balance of power. The structure of the world being what it is today, means the acknowledgment of American power and the prudent will to use it.

In *The Pirates of Penzance*, lyricist W. S. Gilbert wrote, "A policeman's lot is not a happy one." Fate has decreed, however, that for the foreseeable future, we are the major bluecoat of the world. We need, however, to stay away from both the Scyla of isolationism and the Charybdis of accepting every military assignment in our increasingly disordered world. At present our military capacity is proportional to our economic and political power. Unfortunately, there are signs that our willingness to maintain and use that power judiciously may be faltering. Nothing could be more *natural* in a liberal republic, yet nothing could be more *threatening* to the peace that we have recently achieved.

■

BIBLIOGRAPHY

Norman Angell, *The Great Illusion*,
New York: C.P. Putnam's Sons, 1939.

David Barash, *The Whisperings Within: Evolution and the Origin of Human Nature*, New York: Penguin Books, 1979.

Julian Benda, *The Treason of the Intellectuals*,
New York: Morrow & Company, 1928.

Edmund Burke, *Reflections on the Revolution in France*,
New York: Bobbs-Merrill Press, 1955.

Philip Caputo, *A Rumor of War*,
New York: Holt, Rinehart & Winston, 1977.

Pat Conroy, *Beach Music,* New York: Doubleday, 1995.

Steven Coont, *The Intruders,*
New York: Penguin Books, 1978.

Michael Crichton, *Rising Sun,*
New York: Ballantine Books, 1992.

Gavan Daws, *Prisoners of the Japanese,*
New York: W. Morrow, 1994.

Carolo D'Este, *Patton: A Genius For War,*
New York: HarperCollins, 1995.

David Eisenhower, *Eisenhower: At War 1943-1945,* New York, Random House, 1986.

Dwight Eisenhower, *Crusade in Europe,* Garden City: Doubleday, 1948.

J. Glenn Gray, *On Understanding Violence Philosophically,* New York, Harper & Row, 1970.

J. Glenn Gray, *The Warriors: Reflections on Men in Battle,* New York: Harper Torchbooks, 1959.

Edward Gibbon, *The History of the Decline and Fall of the Roman Empire,* London: Dent & Dutton, 1974.

W. E. B. Griffin, *The Corps: Semper FI,* New York: Jove Books, 1986.

Stephen Haseler, *The Varieties of Anti-Americanism,* Washington: Ethics and Public Policy Center, 1985.

Eric Hoffer, *The True Believer,* New York: Harper & Row, 1951.

Joseph P. Lash, *Roosevelt and Churchill, 1939-1941: The Partnership That Saved the West,* New York: Norton, 1976.

Donald Kagan, *On The Origins of War,* New York: Anchor, 1995.

John Keats, *They Fought Alone*,
Philadelphia: Lippencott, 1963.

Eric Lomax, *The Railway Man*,
New York: W. W. Norton, 1995.

William Manchester, *American Caesar: Douglas MacArthur, 1880-1964*, Boston: Little, Brown and Company, 1978.

Karl Mannheim, *Ideology and Utopia*,
New York: Trench, Trubner & Co., 1936.

Robert S. McNamara, *In Retrospect: The Tragedy and Lessons of Vietnam*, New York: Times Books, 1992.

Reinhold Niebuhr, *Leaves From the Notebooks of a Tamed Cynic*, New York: World Publishing Co., 1957.

Reinhold Niebuhr, *Moral Man and Immoral Society*,
New York: Charles Scribner's Sons, 1932.

Reinhold Niebuhr, *The Nature and Destiny of Man*,
New York: Charles Scribner's Sons, 1953.

Yukio Noguchi, *The 1940 System*,
Tokyo: Toyo Keizai Shinposha, 1995.

P. J. O'Rourke, *Give War A Chance*,
New York: The Atlantic Monthly Press, 1992.

Blaise Pascal, *Pensees*, New York: E.P.Dutton & Co., 1958.

George S. Patton, Jr. *War As I Knew It,*
New York: Houghton Mifflin, 1945.

Colin Powell, *My American Journey,*
New York: Random House, 1995.

Charles A. Reich, *The Greening of America,*
New York: Random House, 1970.

Siegfried Sassoon, *The War Poems of Siegfried Sassoon*
London: Heinemann, 1919

Roger Shinn, *War and Rumor of War,*
Nashville: Abingdon Press, 1972.

William L. Shirer, *The Nightmare Years,* 1930-1940,
New York: Simon and Schuster, 1960.

William L. Shirer, *The Rise and Fall of the Third Reich,*
Simon and Schuster, 1959.

B.F. Skinner, *Walden II,* Toronto: Macmillan and Co., 1948.

H. Norman Schwarzkopf, *It Doesn't Take A Hero,*
New York: Linda Gray Bantam Books, 1992.

Thomas Sowell, *The Vision of the Anointed: Self-Congratulation as a Basis for Social Policy,*
New York: Basic Books, 1995.

George W. Stocking, Jr, ed., *Romantic Motives: Essays on Anthropological Sensibility,*
Madison:University of Wisconsin Press, 1989.

Ronald Takak, *Hiroshima: Why America Dropped the Atomic Bomb,* Boston: Little, Brown & Co., 1995.

James Webb, *A Sense of Honor,*
Englewood Cliffs, N.J.: Prentice Hall, 1981.

Stanley Weintraub, *The Last Great Cause: The Intellectuals and the Spanish Civil War,*
New York: Weybright & Talley, 1968.

Leon Wolff, *In Flanders Fields: The 1917 Campaign,*
New York: Time Incorporated, 1958.

Index

A Rumor of War, 146
A Sense of Honor, 149
Aftermath, March 1919, 161
Alton, Bob, 44
American Caesar, 133
Amerika, 92
Amir, Yigal, 190
Ammo, 30- or 50-caliber, 52
An Officer and a Gentleman, 147
Anderson, Tom, 110
Angell, Norman, 224
Animal House, 40
Apocalypse Now, 130
Archie Bunker, 120
Aristotle, 180
Arlington Cemetery, 91
"As a" syndrome, 184
Augustine , 180
Austria, 11
Bailey, President Richard, 125
Baldwin, Stanley, 226
Barash, David, 203
Battle of Bataan, 170
Battle of the Bulge, 138
Beach Music, 104
Benda, Julian, 179
Benedictine Rule, 152
Benjamin, Bob, 8
Bernhardi, 182
Bill Clinton, 92

Blumenthal, Michael, 167
Bly, Robert, 124
Bonhoeffer, Dietrich, 4
Boot Camp, 25
Borah, William, 225
Brothers Karamazov, The, 179
Browning, the Reverend Edmund, 213
Budden, Russell, 42
Burke, Edmund, 185
Bushido, the "Way of the Warrior", 194
Caesar, Julius, 166
Caius Marius , 166
Camp Kearney, 62
Camp, Wayne, 111
Camus, Albert, 87
Caputo, Philip, 137
Carlyle, 91
Cat fever, 61
Chamberlain, Neville, 13, 227
Chaplains, 36
Cheney, Lynne V., 186
Children of Darkness , 175
Children of Light, 175
Christian Century, The, 216
Churchill, Winston, 227
Civil War, 164
Clancy, Tom, 149
Code, 44
Comfort women, 199
Conroy, Pat, 104
Consciousness I, 96
Coont, Steven, 153
Corporate State, 98

Corpus Christianum, 181
Crichton, Michael, 200
Crusade In Europe, 170
Czechoslovakia, 11
D-Day , 138
Daws, Gavin, 197
Daytona Beach, 53
Desert Storm, 215
Dostoevski, 179
Douglass, Frederick, 216
Drill instructor (D.I.), 28
Drucker, Peter, 200
D'Este, Carolo, 136
E pluribus unum, 116
Einstein, Albert, 13
Eisenhower, Dwight, 112
Emperor Hirohito, 194
Enigma of Japanese Power, The, 200
Etzioni, Amitai, 152
Evangelical Protestants, 218
Farewell to Arms, 11
Flanders Fields, 91
Flavius Vegetius, 223
flower-children, 95
Franklin, Benjamin, 97
Freud, 204
Frost, Robert, 119
G.I. Bill, 15
Gandhi , 158
Geschichte, 8
Gibbon, Sir Edward, 99
Gibson, Kenneth, 70
Give War A Chance, 105

Good Samaritan, 156
Graham, Billy, 214
Grant, Ulysses S., 172
Gray, J. Glenn, 87
Great Constructors, the, 207
Great Depression, 97
Great Illusion, The, 224
Griffin, W.E.B., 149
Hamlet, 189
Hamline University, 83
Haseler, Stephen, 101
Hayek. Friedrich, 201
Hemingway, 11
Hess, Ruth, 62
Hiroshima, 14
Hiroshima: Why America Dropped the Atomic Bomb, 196
History of Decline and Fall of the Roman Empire, 99
Hitler, 11
Hobbes, Thomas, 226
Hoffer, Eric, 121
Holmes, Jr., Oliver Wendell, 135
Holocaust, 217
Homer's Iliad, 91
Homo furens, 135
Homosexuals, 171
Hope, Bob, 46
Hull, Cordell, 192
Human Genome Project, 212
Hussein, Saddam, 216
Ideology and Utopia, 148
"Impossible possibility", 219
Industrial Revolution, 95
International Morse Code, 42

Iron John, 126
Ivy League schools, 147
Jackson, Jesse, 216
Jacksonville, 52
Japan, 11
Japan as Number One, 200
Johnson, Andrew, 172
Johnson, Chalmers, 200
Johnson, Fred, 32
Johnson, Lyndon, 125
Just war, 15
Kallsen, Les, 44
Kant, 160
Keats, John, 195
Kee Nee Moo Sha, 56
Kellogg, Franklin, 225
Kellogg-Briand Peace Pact, 225
Kennedy, Bobby, 163
Kennedy, Paul, 200
Kennedy, President, 167
Keynes, John Maynard, 201
Killer instinct, 29
King, Admiral E. J., 192
King, Coretta Scott, 216
King, Martin Luther, 158
Kissinger, Henry, 175
Knox, Frank, 192
Kuwait, 218
Kyser, Kay, 46
Land, Richard, 216
Lasch, Christopher, 152
Law of Unintended Consequences, 188
League of Nations, 11

Leaves From the Notebooks of a Tamed Cynic, 154
Lee, Robert E., 5
Life insurance, 29
Lifton, Robert Jay, 196
Lincoln, Abraham, 4
Lindbergh, Charles, 12
Lorenz, Konrad, 207
Love
    Agape, 142
    Eros, 142
    Philia, 142
    Storge, 142
Luddite tendencies, 102
MacArthur, Douglas, 133
Maginot Line, 228
Mainline churches, 215
Manchester, William, 133
Mannheim, Karl, 148
Marines, 111
Marshall, General George C., 163
Mein Kampf, 226
Memphis, 34
"Men of words", 185
Milwaukee Railroad, 24
Mitchell Convalescent Hospital, 66
MITI and the Japanese Miracle, 200
Monforty, Captain J. C., 39
Moral Man and Immoral Society, 87
Mulkern, Dick, 113
Mussolini, 11
My American Journey, 150
Mysterium Tremendum, 205
Nagasaki, 14

Napoleon, 145
National Council of Churches, 216
National History Standards , 186
Navy Air Corps, 8
Navy hymn, 35
Nazis, 115
New Deal, 97
New Realities, The, 200
Niebuhr, Reinhold, 87
Nihilism, 46
1940 System, 200
Noguchi, Yukio, 200
Nomenclature, 27
Northern Pacific, 74
O'Rourke, P. J., 105
Operation Desert Storm, 117
Orwell, George, 160
Pacifism
    Classical, 156
    Prudential, 156
    Vocational, 156
Pascal, 211
Patton, General George S., 132
Patton: A Genius for War, 150
Peace campaigns, 160
"Peace with Justice", 218
Pearl Harbor, 14
Pennel, John, 111
Pensacola, 45
Peterson, Steve, 110
Picasso, 160
PIIGS--Polish, Irish, Italian, Greek, Slav, 107
Pipestone, Minnesota, 3

Pirates of Penzance, The, 229
Plato, 132
Politically correct, 10
Popenone, David, 148
Powell, Colin, 132
Presidential Scholars, 119
Prisoners of the Japanese, 197
Privateer, 57
Rabin, Yitzhak, 190
Radar, 43
Railway Man, The, 197
Reflections on the Revolution in France, 186
Regan, Tim, 23
Reich, Charles, 95
Rendezvous, 129
Retributive justice, 200
Revisionist historians, 116
Revolution, Violence, and Conscience, 110
Rise and Fall of the Great Powers, The, 200
Rising Sun, 200
Roman Empire, 11
Romantic nationalism, 183
Roosevelt, Franklin D., 12
Rosseau, 95
ROTC programs, 117
Saltpeter, 40
Sartor Resartus, 156
Sassoon, Siegfried, 136
Scale of Being, 205
Schwarzkopf, Norman, 112
Second World War, 7
Seeger, Alan, 129

Sentimentality, 159
Shinn, Roger, 149
Shore Patrolman school, 70
Sign, 115
Skeet shooting, 43
Skinner, 204
Skippy, 39
Social Darwinians, 181
Sociobiology, 203
Sodom and Gomorrah, 26
Sowell, Thomas, 188
SP, 77
Spanish Civil War, 11
Spanish fly, 41
Spit and Argue Club, 68
St. Augustine, 162
St. Paul, 181
Stalin, 158
Stevenson, Adlai, 187
Stockholm Peace Appeal, 160
Students for a Democratic Society, 99
Sunday, 34
Symbol, 115
Sympathetic Magic, 167
Takaki, Ronald, 196
Thanksgiving, 38
The Deer Hunter, 130
The Establishment, 104
The Federalist, 13
The Greening of America, 95
The Hardhat Philosophy of Life, 119
The Intruders, 153
The Pipestone Star, 30

The Plague, 87, 228
The Red Badge of Courage, 132
The Republic, 132
The Varieties of Anti-Americanism, 101
The Warriors: Reflections On Men In Battle, 136
They Fought Alone, 195
Third Reich, 12
Thomas Aquinas , 180
Tillich, Paul, 115
Tojo, 170
Trap shooting, 43
Treason of the Intellectuals (La Trahison des Clercs), The, 179
Tribe of Benjamin, 8
Truman, Capt. Harry S., 137
Tsuneishi, Keiichi, 199
Uemura, Dr. Joseph, 117
Ulysses S. Grant, 172
Uncle Mac, 66
Undertanding Violence Philosophically, On, 87
United Methodists , 215
van Wolferen, Karl, 200
VD, 34
Victorian mores, 34
Viet Cong, 110
Vietnam War, 137
Vision of the Anointed, The, 188
Vogel, Ezra, 200
Voltaire, 199
Vox populi, vox Dei , 220
Walden II, 100
Walker, Jeanne, 73
Wall, James, 216

War and Rumor of War, 149
Webb, James, 149
Whisperings Within, The, 208
Will, George, 91
Williamson, Dr. Arthur, 83
Wilson, Woodrow, 158
Winston, Preston, 37
Wolfe, Tom, 152
Wood, Grant, 96
World Council of Churches, 218
World War I, 136
Wycliffe, John, 183
Xenophobia, 181
Yellow Water, 52

NOTES

NOTES

NOTES

NOTES

NOTES

NOTES

NOTES

NOTES

NOTES

ORDER FORM

Red Oak Press
Box 10614
White Bear Lake MN 55110-0614

Please send _____ copies of *War and Reflection* to:

_____

_____

_____

Enclosed is our check for $_____ ($15.95 per copy including tax, shipping and handling.

(You may also order in any of the following ways):

TEL: 612-426-5704

FAX: 612-426-7039   internet:72317.1206@compuserve.com